# English-German
## Glossary of Namibian Terms

Edited by
Marianne Zappen-Thomson

with
Heide Beinhauer, Hella Eichhoff, Heide Grassmann,
Hanne Hügel, Andrea Lowe, Regine von Teichmann

**UNAM PRESS**
UNIVERSITY OF NAMIBIA

University of Namibia Press
Private Bag 13301
Windhoek
Namibia


© Marianne Zappen-Thomson, 2012
All rights reserved. No part of this publication may be reproduced, stored in any retrieval system or transmitted in any form, or by any means, e.g. electronic, mechanical, photocopying, recording or otherwise without prior permission of the author.

First Published:     2012
Design and layout:   John Meinert Printers, Windhoek
Printed by:          John Meinert Printers, Windhoek


ISBN: 978-99916-42-03-1

Distribution:
In Namibia by Demasius Publications: www.demasius-publications.com
In the rest of Southern Africa by Blue Weaver: www.blueweaver.co.za
Internationally by the African Books Collective: www.africanbookscollective.com

# Contents

Preface .................................................................................................. iv

Vorwort ................................................................................................ vi

## English – German
Schools and Administration ........................................................... 2
Everyday Politics and Ministries ................................................... 15
Law and Related Matters .............................................................. 24
Special Education .......................................................................... 28
Gender Issues ................................................................................ 34

## Deutsch – Englisch
Schule und Schulverwaltung ........................................................ 42
Alltagspolitik und Ministerien ...................................................... 58
Rechtswesen .................................................................................. 68
Sonderpädagogik ........................................................................... 73
Geschlechterfragen ....................................................................... 80

# Preface

Since Namibia's independence in 1990 a variety of new English words have come into use which refer predominantly to the political developments but also to changes in society in general.

As German is one of the national languages in Namibia, the changes in society have to be expressed in this language as well. As these changes are unique to the Namibian context, very often equivalent words cannot be found in existing German dictionaries. During their course of study for the Postgraduate Diploma in Translation (PGDT) at the University of Namibia (UNAM) from 2006 to 2007 a group of students became acutely aware of this.

The students soon defined their fields of interest and started collecting English terminology concerning education, government ministries, special education, law and gender related topics for which no adequate equivalent exists in the German language. During intense working sessions and in collaboration with colleagues of the German Section at the University of Namibia, the University of Duisburg-Essen and the University of Bonn, terminology was coined to express as accurately as possible the given English vocabulary in German. After this process it had to be verified and standardised. This was not easily done since no official standard Namibian-German vocabulary exists as yet. Therefore there is an urgent need for this glossary in order to standardise the use of terminology in the Namibian-German media as well as in schools.

The aim of this glossary is not to duplicate what can be found in existing dictionaries but rather to expand them, keeping in mind the need for the appropriate translation of a terminology that is unique and specific to Namibia.

The first part of the glossary is English-German, as this is the part that is of greatest importance. In order to make the glossary more user-friendly though, it also has a German-English part.

This glossary is intended for the German speaking community in Namibia, in particular for use by the German radio services, the *Allgemeine Zeitung*, schools where German is taught as mother tongue as well as a foreign language, and for students at UNAM. Furthermore it is intended for researchers in various fields who need to refer to specific topics in German. This book could also serve as a basis for other national languages in Namibia faced with the same problem.

I would like to thank my colleagues Hans-Volker Gretschel, Jörg Klinner, Dieter Faulhaber, Katrin Krüger and Christoph Chlosta for their input. Without the help of members of the *Arbeitsgemeinschaft Deutscher Schulvereine* (AGDS), the *Allgemeine Zeitung* and the German Radio Service of the Namibian Broadcasting Corporation (NBC) this process would not have been possible.

This glossary is a work-in-progress since language develops as society develops. I will strive to expand the range of topics in future and would be very grateful for any suggestions.

Last but not least I would like to thank the University of Namibia, particularly Jane Katjavivi and her team from UNAM Press, for their professional advice and support. I am extremely grateful to them.

*Marianne Zappen-Thomson*

# Vorwort

Ebenso wie sich das Leben in Namibia nach der Unabhängigkeit 1990 verändert hat, hat sich auch die Amtssprache Englisch gewandelt. Neue Institutionen sind ins Leben gerufen worden, neue Begebenheiten eingetreten, und für diese sind neue englische Begriffe entstanden. Da Deutsch eine der namibischen Landessprachen ist, muss es für diese neuen Begriffe auch angemessene Übersetzungen geben.

Es hat sich schnell gezeigt, dass Wörterbücher aus den deutschsprachigen Ländern Europas häufig kein angemessenes Äquivalent für die neue namibische Terminologie bieten können, da die Realitäten dort anders sind. Dies ist einer Gruppe von Studierenden, die 2006/7 das Postgraduate Diploma in Translation (PGDT) an der Universität Namibia erworben haben, besonders aufgefallen.

Aus diesem Bedarf heraus ist dieses Projekt entstanden. Die Studierenden legten zunächst verschiedene Interessengebiete fest, nämlich Schule, Ministerien, politischer Alltag, Rechtswesen, Sonderpädagogik und Geschlechterfragen. Dann sammelten sie englische Begriffe, für die es kein angemessenes deutsches Äquivalent gab. In Zusammenarbeit mit den KollegInnen der Sektion Deutsch der Universität Namibia und den Universitäten Duisburg-Essen und Bonn wurden neue deutsche Begriffe erarbeitet. Da es für Namibia noch kein standardisiertes Deutsch gibt, war dieser Prozess dringend erforderlich, erwies sich aber durchaus auch als schwierig.

Ziel dieses Glossars ist, zu einem einheitlichen Sprachgebrauch innerhalb Namibias beizutragen, zumindest für die oben genannten Themenbereiche. Das es bislang keine solchen Richtlinien gab, ging man mit Übersetzungen eher willkürlich um, was immer wieder zu Verwirrung führte. Das Glossar versteht sich daher als eine notwendige Ergänzung zu existierenden Wörterbüchern und will diese keineswegs ersetzen.

Auf Grund der skizzierten Situation steht der Teil Englisch-Deutsch am Anfang des Glossars, gefolgt vom Deutsch-Englisch Teil.

Die vorrangige Zielgruppe des Glossars ist die Deutsch sprechende Gemeinschaft Namibias. Im Besonderen soll das Glossar in den deutschen Medien wie der Allgemeinen Zeitung, den deutschen Hörfunkprogrammen sowie den Schulen benutzt werden. Selbstverständlich wird es aber auch Wissenschaftlern sowie Vertretern verschiedener Nicht-Regierungsorganisationen wichtige Dienste leisten können. Da andere nationale Sprachen Namibias vor dem gleichen Problem der fehlenden Terminologien in ihren Sprachen stehen, wäre es besonders erfreulich, wenn dieses Glossar die Grundlage für weitere Glossare bilden würde.

Meinen KollegInnen Hans-Volker Gretschel, Jörg Klinner, Dieter Faulhaber, Katrin Krüger und Christoph Chlosta danke ich für kritische Anmerkungen, Geduld und Unterstützung. Ohne die Hilfe der Arbeitsgemeinschaft Deutscher Schulvereine (AGDS), der Allgemeinen Zeitung und des Deutschen Hörfunkprogramms (DHFP) der NBC (Namibische Rundfunkgesellschaft) wäre das Glossar ein Traum geblieben.

Die Arbeit an einem solchen Glossar ist nie abgeschlossen, daher werde ich weiterhin an der Terminologie feilen und die Themenliste erweitern. Dazu aber brauche ich die Unterstützung der BenutzerInnen dieses Glossars und freue mich über alle Anmerkungen und Hinweise.

Ein ganz besonderer Dank geht an die Universität Namibia, vor allem an Jane Katjavivi und ihr Team der UNAM Press, die aus der Idee ein Buch haben werden lassen. Danke!

*Marianne Zappen-Thomson*

# English-German

# Schools and Administration | Schule und Schulverwaltung

## A

| | |
|---|---|
| academic progress | akademischer/schulischer Fortschritt |
| access test, entrance exam | Aufnahmeprüfung, Zulassungsprüfung |
| admission of learners not based on race, ethnic origin or colour and creed | Zulassung, Aufnahme von Lernenden, ungeachtet der Rasse, Hautfarbe, ethnischer oder konfessioneller Zugehörigkeit |
| admission refused | Zulassung verweigert/verwehrt/nicht genehmigt/abgelehnt |
| admission requirements | Zulassungsbedingungen |
| adult education | Erwachsenenbildung |
| advanced technical certificate | Fachhochschulreife |
| advisory committee/council | Beirat |
| aid for private schools | Subventionierung privater Schulen |
| aims and objectives | Lernziele |
| alumni, former students, alumnus, alumna | Altschüler(innen), ehemalige Lernende, Alumni, Alumnus, Alumna |
| annual school calendar | Schulterminkalender |
| application | Antrag, Bewerbung |
| application for admission | Zulassungsantrag, Aufnahmeantrag |
| application form | Anmeldeformular |
| approach | Ansatz, Vorgehensweise, Einführung |
| aptitude test | Eignungstest (Universität) |
| assessing competence | Befugnis, Befähigung zur Leistungseinschätzung |
| assessment | Beurteilung, Bewertung, Leistungseinschätzung |
| assessment form | Beurteilungsformular, -bogen |

## B

| | |
|---|---|
| board of directors, school board | Vorstand |
| board of examiners | Prüfungsausschuss |
| boarding fees | Heimgebühren |
| boarding school | Schule mit Schülerheim |
| Bursar (UNAM) | Finanzverwalter(in) |

## C

| | |
|---|---|
| career guidance | Berufsberatung |
| certificate | Zertifikat, Zeugnis, Attest, Bescheinigung |
| Chancellor (of the University of Namibia) | Universitätspräsident(in) |
| change of teaching methods | Methodenwechsel (didaktischer) |
| chief examiner | Hauptprüfungsbeauftragte(r) |
| class outing | Klassenausflug, Klassenfahrt |
| class teaching | Klassenunterricht |
| class test | Klassenarbeit, Test |
| classification of state schools and hostels | Einstufung der Staatsschulen und Heime |
| code of conduct | Verhaltensregel, Verhaltenskodex |
| coeducation | Koedukation, gemeinsamer Unterricht von Jungen und Mädchen |
| combined school | Schule mit Primar- und Sekundarstufe |
| committee | Komitee, Gremium, Ausschuss |
| compulsory school attendance | Schulpflicht |
| computer science | Informatik |
| concept of support for the junior secondary grades | Förderkonzept für die Sekundarstufe I |
| concept of support for the primary grades | Förderkonzept für die Primarstufe |

| | |
|---|---|
| conditions for admission | Zulassungsbedingungen |
| conditions of registration | Anmeldebestimmungen |
| conference | Konferenz |
| confidante | Vertrauenslehrer(in) |
| constitute a quorum (to) | beschlussfähig sein (Versammlung) |
| Content and Language Integrated Learning in German (CLIL) | Deutscher Fachunterricht (DFU) |
| contribution by parents | Beitrag der Eltern, Elternanteil |
| controlling body of a school | Aufsichtsgremium einer Schule, Schulaufsichtsgremium, Schulvorstand |
| core curriculum | Basislehrplan, Kernlehrplan, verbindlicher Lehrplan |
| contact school | Begegnungsschule |
| corporal punishment | Prügelstrafe, körperliche Züchtigung |
| correct (to) | korrigieren |
| course of study | Studiengang |
| criteria of support | Förderrahmen (finanziell) |
| curriculum | Curriculum, Lehrplan |
| curriculum development | Lehrplanentwicklung |

## D

| | |
|---|---|
| day-care hostel/centre | Tagesheim |
| diploma | Diplom, Zeugnis, Urkunde |
| disciplinary hearing | Disziplinarverfahren |
| disciplinary conference | Disziplinarkonferenz |
| distance education | Fernstudium |
| documentary evidence | Urkundenbeweis, dokumentarischer Nachweis |
| draft examination paper | Prüfungsvorschlag, Prüfungsentwurf |
| dyscalculia | Dyskalkulie, Rechenschwäche |
| dyslexia | Legasthenie, Lese- und Rechtschreibschwäche |

# E

| | |
|---|---|
| education | Ausbildung, Bildung, Erziehung |
| Education and Training Sector Improvement Programme (ETSIP) | Programm zur Verbesserung des Schul- und Ausbildungsbereichs |
| education crisis | Bildungskrise, -notstand |
| education officer | Beamter (Beamtin) des Bildungsministeriums |
| education policy, educational policy | Bildungspolitik, Schulpolitik, Bildungsrichtlinien |
| education system | Bildungssystem, Erziehungssystem |
| educational establishment/institution | Bildungsanstalt, -einrichtung, -stätte |
| educational level | Bildungsstufe, Bildungsstand, Bildungsniveau |
| educational material | Unterrichtsmaterialien |
| educational opportunities | Bildungschancen |
| educational reform | Bildungsreform |
| educational theory | Lehr- und Lerntheorie, Pädagogik, Erziehungstheorie |
| empower (to) | befähigen, ermächtigen, befugt sein zu |
| English Medium Branch | englischsprachiger Zweig, Neue Sekundarstufe |
| evaluate (to) | bewerten, beurteilen, auswerten |
| evaluation | Bewertung, Evaluation, Beurteilung, Einschätzung, Auswertung |
| exam, examination | Prüfung, Klausur, Examen |
| examination paper | Prüfungsbogen, Examensbogen, Fragebogen |
| examination regulations | Prüfungsordnung |
| examiner | Prüfer(in), Examinator(in) |
| examining body | Prüfungsausschuss, Examensausschuss |
| exemption from payment | Gebührenbefreiung |
| exemption for universities | Universitätsreife |

| | |
|---|---|
| exemption for universities of applied sciences | Fachhochschulreife |
| expulsion/suspension of a learner | Schulverweis, Schulausschluss, Suspendierung |
| extra classes, extra lessons | zusätzlicher Unterricht |
| extracurricular | außerschulisch, außerhalb des Lehr-/Stundenplans |
| extracurricular activity | außerschulische Veranstaltung, Arbeitsgemeinschaft (AG) |

## F

| | |
|---|---|
| Federal Office of Administration | Bundesverwaltungsamt |
| federal programme teacher, seconded teacher | Bundesprogrammlehrkraft (BPLK) |
| field of study | Studienrichtung |
| fill in a form (to) | ein Formular ausfüllen |
| final examination | Abschlussprüfung |
| fine motor skills | Feinmotorik |
| form of assessment | Art und Weise der Beurteilung |
| free learning aids | kostenlose/kostenfreie Lernmittel, Lernmittelfreiheit |
| fully acknowledged Senior Secondary School Leaving Certificate | (vollgültiger) Sekundarschulabschluss in Namibia |

## G

| | |
|---|---|
| general education | Allgemeinbildung |
| general rules of behaviour/conduct | allgemeine Verhaltensregeln, Verhaltenskodex |
| German Language Diploma | Deutsches Sprachdiplom |
| grade | Klasse, Note |
| grade (to) | benoten, zensieren |
| grade rating | Noteneinstufung |
| grade review | Anpassung der Noten an die Gaußsche Normalverteilungskurve |

| | |
|---|---|
| grade threshold | Notenschwellenwert, Schwellenwert bei Noteneinstufung |
| graduate (to) | graduieren |
| graduate | Absolvent(in), Graduierte(r) |
| gross motor skills | Grobmotorik |

## H

| | |
|---|---|
| Head of Cultural Affairs/Cultural Desk | Kulturreferent(in) (Botschaft), Leiter(in) der Kulturabteilung |
| head of department (primary, secondary school) | Stufenleiter(in), Abteilungsleiter(in) |
| headmaster, principal, headmistress | Schulleiter(in), Schuldirektor(in) |
| hidden curriculum | heimlicher Lehrplan |
| higher education, university education | akademische Bildung, Hochschulbildung, Universitätsausbildung |
| home schooling | Unterricht zu Hause, Home Schooling, Hausunterricht |
| hostel | Schülerheim (Internat) |
| hostel committee | Heimausschuss |
| hostel management | Heimleitung |
| hostel parents' representative council | Heimelternvertretung |
| house rules | Hausordnung |

## I

| | |
|---|---|
| inclusive education | integrative Erziehung, inklusive Pädagogik |
| indemnity form | Haftungsausschlussformular |
| informal learning | informelles/formloses/zwangloses Lernen |
| in-service teacher training | berufsbegleitende Lehrerfortbildung |
| institutional framework requirements | institutionelle Rahmenbedingungen |
| intern | Praktikant(in) |
| internship | Praktikum, Referendariat |

## J

| | |
|---|---|
| junior education | Vor- und Grundschulerziehung |
| junior secondary school | Sekundarstufe I |

## L

| | |
|---|---|
| lateral entrant, transfer student | Seiteneinsteiger(in) |
| learner support | Förderung/Unterstützung von Lernenden |
| learners' code of conduct | Verhaltensregeln, -kodex für Lernende |
| learner | Lernende(r), Schüler(in), Lerner(in) |
| learners' representative council | Schülermitverantwortung (SMV), Schülervertretung, Schülermitverwaltung |
| learning achievement | Lernerfolg |
| learning by doing | Learning by Doing, handelnd lernen, praktisches Lernen |
| learning content | Lerninhalte |
| learning evaluation | Lernerfolgskontrolle |
| learning method | Lernmethode |
| learning process | Lernprozess |
| learning types | Lerntypen |
| learning and teaching aids | Lern- und Lehrmittel |
| learning-disabled, slow learner | lernbehindert, Lernende(r) mit Lernstörungen |
| leaving certificate | Abgangszeugnis |
| lecture | Vorlesung |
| lecturer | Dozent(in), Hochschullehrende(r) |
| lesson objective | Unterrichtsziel, Stundenziel |
| lesson plan | Unterrichtsplan, Unterrichtsentwurf |
| lesson preparation | Unterrichtsvorbereitung |
| letter of acceptance | schriftliche Zusage |
| liaison teacher | Vertrauenslehrer(in) |

| | |
|---|---|
| literacy campaign | Alphabetisierungskampagne |
| local teacher | Ortslehrkraft (OLK) |

| | |
|---|---|
| marker's comments | Anmerkungen des Prüfers (der Prüferin) |
| mark (to) | korrigieren, zensieren |
| marking scheme | Bewertungsschema, -matrix, Erwartungshorizont |
| Matriculation Exemption | Universitätsreife, Universitätszulassungsberechtigung, Immatrikulationsberechtigung *(kann sich an einer Universität immatrikulieren lassen)* |
| media in teaching | Medien im Unterricht |
| medium of instruction | Unterrichtssprache |
| mentor | Mentor |
| methodology | Methodik |
| minimum requirements | Mindestanforderungen |
| minimum standards | Mindeststandard, Mindestniveau, Mindestnorm |
| Ministry of Education | Bildungsministerium |
| misconduct | Fehlverhalten |
| mission statement | Leitbild |
| moderate (to) | gegenlesen, bestätigen |
| moderator | Zweitkorrektor(in), Zweitprüfer(in) |
| module | Modul |
| multi-purpose sports field | Multiplatz |

| | |
|---|---|
| Namibian National Teachers Union (NANTU) | Namibische Nationale Lehrergewerkschaft |
| Namibia Senior Secondary Certificate (NSSC) | NSSC-Abschluss (Namibisches Sekundarstufen-Zertifikat) |

| | |
|---|---|
| New Primary School | Neue Primarstufe |
| notice of warning | schriftlicher Verweis |

## O

| | |
|---|---|
| open learning | Offener Unterricht (OU), Freiarbeit |
| oral examination | mündliche Prüfung |

## P

| | |
|---|---|
| parents' representative council | Elternbeirat |
| parents' representative | Elternvertreter(in) |
| parents meeting | Elternversammlung |
| parents evening | Elternabend |
| payment of tuition, tuition fees | Zahlung der Unterrichtsgebühren, Schulgeld |
| pedagogical/educational advisory board | Pädagogischer Beirat |
| Polytechnic of Namibia (PON) | Polytechnikum Namibia |
| practical teaching | Unterrichtspraktikum, Unterricht während des Referendariats, praktischer Unterricht |
| price-performance ratio | Preis-Leistungs-Verhältnis |
| primary education | Grundschulausbildung, Primarstufenbildung |
| primary school | Grundschule |
| principal | Schulleiter(in), Schuldirektor(in) |
| principal's office | Büro des Schulleiters (der Schulleiterin) |
| private lessons | Privatunterricht, Nachhilfeunterricht |
| private school | Privatschule |
| private tuition | Privatunterricht, Privatstunden |
| professional standards for teachers | Berufsrichtlinien für Lehrer(innen), Lehrende |
| professional studies | Fachstudium |
| project work | Projektarbeit |

| | |
|---|---|
| proofreading of examination papers/ scripts | Korrekturlesen der Prüfungsbögen/ Prüfungsarbeiten |
| provision of materials | Ausstattung mit Unterrichtsmaterial, Lehrmittelbereitstellung |
| Pro-Vice-Chancellor | Konrektor(in), Prorektor(in) |
| provision of teachers | Verfügbarkeit von Lehrenden, Zuteilung von Lehrkräften |
| pupil | Lerner(in), Lernende(r), Schüler(in) |

## Q

| | |
|---|---|
| question paper | Prüfungsbogen, Aufgabenblatt |

## R

| | |
|---|---|
| reduction of school fees | Schulgeldermäßigung |
| Regional Education Forum | Regionaler Erziehungsausschuss, Erziehungs- und Bildungsausschuss der Region, Regionales Bildungsforum |
| regional training course | ReFo (Regionale Fortbildung) |
| Registrar | Registrar(in), Registrator(in) |
| registration | Registrierung, Anmeldung, Einschreibung, Immatrikulation |
| remedial teaching/education | Förderunterricht |
| report | Zeugnis, Bericht |

## S

| | |
|---|---|
| school administration | Schulverwaltung |
| school attendance | Anwesenheit |
| school board | Schulvorstand, -komitee |
| school clinic | Schulklinik |
| school development | Schulentwicklung |
| school development fund | Schulfonds, Schulentwicklungsfonds |
| school management | Schulleitung, Schulverwaltung |
| school readiness test | Schulreifetest, Einschulungstest |
| school report | Zeugnis, Schulzeugnis |

| | |
|---|---|
| school subsidy | Schulbeihilfe, Zuschuss |
| school-based training for teachers | Schilf (Schulinterne Lehrerfortbildung) |
| secondary school | Oberstufe(nschule), Sekundarstufe I und II |
| secondary education | Sekundarschulwesen |
| secretary | Protokollführer(in) |
| self-responsible learning, learning independently | Eigenverantwortliches Arbeiten (EVA) |
| senior secondary school | Sekundarstufe II, Oberstufe |
| service company | Dienstleistungsbetrieb |
| short test | Kurztest |
| sit in (to) | hospitieren |
| special course of study | bestimmte Fachrichtung |
| special education | Sonderpädagogik |
| special school | Sonderschule, Förderschule |
| staff matters | Personalangelegenheiten, -fragen |
| staff meeting | Lehrerkonferenz (Gesamtkonferenz, GLK) |
| staff (members) | Kollegium |
| staff room | Lehrerzimmer |
| Standing Conference of the Ministers of Education and Cultural Affairs of the Länder (federal states) in the Federal Republic of Germany | Ständige Konferenz der Kultusminister der Länder in der Bundesrepublik Deutschland (Kultusministerkonferenz, KMK) |
| state school, government school | Staatsschule, Regierungsschule, staatliche Schule |
| steering committee | Lenkungsausschuss |
| student | Studierende(r), Student(in), Lerner(in), Lernende(r) |
| student teacher | Lehramtsanwärter(in), Referendar(in) |
| study institution | Studieneinrichtung |
| study | Studium |
| study (to) | studieren |
| subject | Fach, Schulfach |

| | |
|---|---|
| subject meeting | Fachkonferenz |
| subject methodology and didactics | Fachdidaktik und –methodik |
| subject teaching | Fachunterricht |
| subsidy of schools | Schulbeihilfe aus öffentlichen Geldern, staatliche Zuwendung für Schulen, Subventionierung der Schulen |
| supervisory council | Aufsichtsrat |
| suspension of learner | Ausschluss eines (einer) Lernenden vom Unterricht, Ausschluss vom Unterricht, Unterrichtsverweis |
| syllabus | Lehrplan, Syllabus, Fachlehrplan |

## T

| | |
|---|---|
| teacher | Lehrer(in), Lehrende(r) |
| teacher abroad | Auslandsdienstlehrkraft (ADLK) |
| teachers resource centre | Lehrmittelzentrum, Mediathek |
| teachers representative committee, teachers advisory board | Lehrerbeirat |
| teaching aids | Lehrmittel |
| teaching competency | Lehrbefähigung, Lehrkompetenz |
| teaching media | Unterrichtsmedien |
| teaching method | Lehrmethode |
| teaching practice | Unterrichtspraktikum, Erfahrung im Unterrichten |
| Teachers Union of Namibia (TUN) | Lehrergewerkschaft Namibias |
| terms and conditions of admission | Aufnahmebedingungen |
| tertiary education | Hochschulbildung, Universitätsbildung, tertiärer Bildungssektor |
| toddlers group | Krabbelgruppe |
| transfer student, lateral entrant | Seiteneinsteiger(in) |
| tuition | Unterricht |
| tuition fees | Unterrichtsgebühren, Schulgeld |

## U

| | |
|---|---|
| undergraduate | Studierende(r) vor dem ersten akademischen Abschluss (Grad)/ohne akademischen Abschluss (Grad) |
| undergraduate studies | Studium bis zum Bachelor-Abschluss |
| university entrance diploma | NSSC-Abschluss, Abitur |
| university exemption | Hochschulzugangsberechtigung, Universitätsreife |
| University of Namibia (UNAM) | Universität Namibia |

## V

| | |
|---|---|
| variety of teaching methods | Methodenvielfalt |
| Vice-Chancellor | Rektor(in) |

## W

| | |
|---|---|
| work experience | Berufserfahrung |
| written examination | schriftliche Prüfung |

# Everyday Politics and Ministries

# Alltagspolitik und Ministerien

## A

| | |
|---|---|
| additional budget | Nachtragshaushalt |
| advisory committee | beratender Ausschuss, Beratungsausschuss, beratendes Gremium |
| affirmative action | aktive Förderungsmaßnahmen, Maßnahmen zur Chancengleichheit, Fördermaßnahmen zugunsten benachteiligter Gruppen, Korrekturmaßnahmen, korrigierende Maßnahmen |
| agriculture | Landwirtschaft, Agrikultur |
| Agricultural Employers Association (AEA) | Landwirtschaftlicher Arbeitgeberverband (LAV) |
| agricultural statistics | Agrarstatistik, Landwirtschaftsstatistik |
| aquaculture, freshwater and marine | Aquakultur |
| Auditor General | Generalbuchprüfer(in), Generalbilanzprüfer(in), Generalwirtschaftsprüfer(in) |

## B

| | |
|---|---|
| baby dumping | Babyentsorgung |
| Bank of Namibia (BoN) | Namibische Zentralbank |
| black economic empowerment | Programm zur Förderung schwarzen Unternehmertums/schwarzer Unternehmer/Firmen/Firmeninhaber; wirtschaftliche Stärkung der schwarzen Bevölkerung |

## C

| | |
|---|---|
| Cancer Association of Namibia (CAN) | Namibische Krebsvereinigung |
| capacity building | Kompetenzförderung, Ausbau von Kapazitäten |

| | |
|---|---|
| Chief | Chief |
| citizenship | Staatsangehörigkeit, Staatsbürgerschaft |
| citizenship documents | amtlicher Nachweis der Staatsangehörigkeit/ Staatsbürgerschaft |
| communal management of rural water supply | ländliche Wasserversorgung |
| community based | auf Gemeindeebene/ Gemeinschaftsebene, gemeindebasiert |
| Council of Churches in Namibia (CCN) | Namibischer Kirchenrat |
| customary land rights | Gewohnheitsrecht auf Grund und Boden |

## D

| | |
|---|---|
| decentralisation process | Dezentralisierungsprozess |
| Department of National Examinations and Assessment (DNEA) | Nationale Prüfungsbehörde |
| disaster control | Katastrophenschutz |
| disaster relief | Katastrophenhilfe |

## E

| | |
|---|---|
| Electoral Commission of Namibia (ECN) | Namibische Wahlkommission |
| economic processing zone | Wirtschaftsbearbeitungszone |
| emergency management unit | Notfallmanagement |
| employees compensation fund | Arbeitnehmerhaftpflichtversicherung |
| employment equity commission | Kommission zur Gleichstellung am Arbeitsplatz |
| exclusive processing zone | ausschließliche Wirtschaftszone |
| export processing zone (EPZ) | Exportverarbeitungszone |
| extension services/officer | Landwirtschaftlicher Beratungsdienst/ Berater(in) |

## F

| | |
|---|---|
| Federation of Namibian Tourism Associations (FENATA) | Namibischer Touristikdachverband |
| fish farming | Fischfarmerei, Fischzucht |

## G

| | |
|---|---|
| Geological Survey of Namibia | Landesamt für Geologie, Geologisches Landesamt |
| Government Institutions Pension Fund (GIPF) | Pensionsfonds staatlicher Institutionen |

## H

| | |
|---|---|
| Hospitality Association of Namibia (HAN) | Namibischer Gastgewerbeverband |
| Heroes Acre | Heldengedenkstätte, Heldenfriedhof |

## I

| | |
|---|---|
| illegal strike | widerrechtlicher/illegaler Streik, wilder Streik |
| Inspector General | Generalinspekteur(in) |
| Institute for Public Policy Research (IPPR) | Institut für Politikforschung |

## J

| | |
|---|---|
| Joint Commission of Culture | Gemeinsame Kulturkommission |
| Joint Commission on Defence and Security | Gemeinsame Verteidigungs- und Sicherheitskommission |

## L

| | |
|---|---|
| labour commission | Arbeitskommission |
| labour commissioner | Beauftragte(r) für Arbeitsrecht, Arbeitskommissar(in) |

| | |
|---|---|
| labour inspector | Arbeitsinspektor(in), Gewerbeaufsichtsperson, Gewerbeaufseher(in) |
| labour inspectorate | Gewerbeaufsichtsamt, Arbeitsaufsichtsamt, Arbeitsaufsichtsbehörde |
| labour legislation | Arbeitsrecht |
| Labour Resource and Research Institute (LaRRI) | Arbeitsforschungsinstitut |
| land board | Behörde/Rat/Ausschuss zur Vergabe von Farmland |
| land policy | Bodenpolitik |
| land reform | Bodenreform |
| land valuation and taxation | Bodenabschätzung und Besteuerung |
| land tax | Farmlandsteuer, Bodensteuer |
| Law Reform and Development Commission of Namibia | Namibische Rechtsreform- und Entwicklungskommission |
| Law Society of Namibia | Namibische Juristenvereinigung |
| Local Authorities Union of Namibia | Namibische Gewerkschaft für Stadtverwaltungsangestellte |

## M

| | |
|---|---|
| media conference | Pressekonferenz |
| Metal and Allied Namibian Workers Union | Namibische Gewerkschaft für Metallindustriearbeiter/ Metallarbeiter(innen) |
| Mine Workers Union of Namibia | Namibische Bergarbeitergewerkschaft |
| Minister of Presidential Affairs | Minister des Präsidialamts/für Präsidentschaftsangelegenheiten |
| Ministry of Agriculture, Water and Forestry | Ministerium für Wasserversorgung, Land- und Forstwirtschaft |
| Ministry of Defence | Verteidigungsministerium |
| Ministry of Education | Bildungsministerium |
| Ministry of Environment and Tourism | Umwelt- und Touristikministerium, Ministerium für Umwelt und Touristik |
| Ministry of Finance | Finanzministerium |

| | |
|---|---|
| Ministry of Fisheries and Marine Resources | Ministerium für Hochseefischerei und Meeresressourcen |
| Ministry of Foreign Affairs | Außenministerium, Auswärtiges Amt |
| Ministry of Gender Equality and Child Welfare | Ministerium für Geschlechtergleichheit und Kinderfürsorge |
| Ministry of Health and Social Services | Ministerium für Gesundheit und Sozialleistungen |
| Ministry of Home Affairs and Immigration | Innenministerium |
| Ministry of Information and Communication Technology | Ministerium für Information und Kommunikationstechnologie |
| Ministry of Justice | Justizministerium |
| Ministry of Labour and Social Welfare | Ministerium für Arbeit und Soziales |
| Ministry of Lands and Resettlement | Ministerium für Landfragen und Neubesiedlung |
| Ministry of Mines and Energy | Ministerium für Bergbau und Energie |
| Ministry of Presidential Affairs | Ministerium des Präsidialamts/für Präsidentschaftsangelegenheiten |
| Ministry of Regional and Local Government, Housing and Rural Development | Ministerium für Kommunal- und Regionalverwaltung, Wohnungsbau und ländliche Entwicklung |
| Ministry of Safety and Security | Ministerium für Innere Sicherheit |
| Ministry of Trade and Industry | Industrie- und Handelsministerium |
| Ministry of Veteran Affairs | Ministerium für Kriegsveteranen |
| Ministry of Works and Transport | Ministerium für öffentliche Arbeiten und Verkehr |
| Ministry of Youth, National Service, Sport and Culture | Ministerium für Jugend, Wehrdienst, Sport und Kultur |
| Motor Vehicle Accident Fund (MVA Fund) | Fahrzeugunfallfonds |

## N

| | |
|---|---|
| Namibia Agricultural Union (NAU) | Namibischer Landwirtschaftsverband |
| Namibia Airport Company (NAC) | Namibische Flughafengesellschaft |
| Namibia Building Workers Union (NABWU) | Namibische Bauarbeitergewerkschaft |

| | |
|---|---|
| Namibia Bus and Taxi Association (NABTA) | Namibische Bus- und Taxivereinigung |
| Namibian Chamber of Commerce and Industry (NCCI) | Namibische Industrie- und Handelskammer |
| Namibia Community Based Tourism Association (NACOBTA) | Namibischer Verband für Touristik auf Gemeindeebene |
| Namibia Farm Workers Union (NAFWU) | Namibische Farmarbeitergewerkschaft |
| Namibia Financial Institutions Supervisory Authority (NAMFISA) | Namibische Kontrollbehörde für Finanzinstitute |
| Namibia Fishing Industries and Fishermen Workers Union (Namfish) | Namibische Fischindustriegewerkschaft |
| Namibia National Farmers Union (NNFU) | Namibischer Verband der Kommunalfarmer |
| Namibia National Teachers Union (NANTU) | Namibische Nationale Lehrergewerkschaft |
| Namibia Non-governmental Organisations Forum Trust (NANGOF Trust) | Dachverband namibischer Nicht-Regierungs-Organisationen |
| Namibia Paralegal Association (NPA) | Namibische Vereinigung der Rechtsassistenten (-innen) |
| Namibia Public Workers Union (NAPWU) | Namibische Gewerkschaft für Angestellte des öffentlichen Dienstes |
| Namibia Professional Hunting Association (NAPHA) | Namibischer Berufsjagdverband |
| Namibia Standards Institution (NSI) | Namibisches Institut für Normung |
| Namibia Tourism Board (NTB) | Namibische Touristikbehörde |
| Namibia Wildlife Resorts (NWR) | Namibische Naturparks |
| Namibia Wholesale and Retail Workers Union (NWRWU) | Namibische Gewerkschaft für Angestellte im Groß- und Einzelhandel |
| Namibian Academy for Tourism and Hospitality (NATH) | Namibische Akademie für Touristik und Gastgewerbe |
| Namibian Defence Force (NDF) | Namibische Verteidigung/Streitkräfte, Streitmacht/Armee |
| Namibian Employers Federation (NEF) | Namibischer Arbeitgeberverband |

| | |
|---|---|
| Namibian Food and Allied Workers Union (NAFAU) | Namibische Gewerkschaft für Angestellte der Nahrungsmittelindustrie |
| Namibian Manufacturers Association (NMA) | Namibischer Produzentenverband |
| Namibian Qualifications Authority (NQA) | Namibische Zentralstelle für die Anerkennung von Bildungsabschlüssen, Namibische Qualifizierungsbehörde |
| Namibian Rights and Responsibilities Inc. (NAMRIGHTS) | Namibische Vereinigung für Recht und Verantwortung |
| Namibian Stock Exchange (NSX) | Namibische Börse |
| National Art Gallery | Nationalgalerie |
| National Archives | Nationalarchiv |
| National Council for Higher Education (NCHE) | Nationaler Hochschulrat |
| National Institute for Educational Development (NIED) | Nationales Institut für Bildungsentwicklung |
| National Library of Namibia | Nationalbibliothek |
| National Museum of Namibia | Nationalmuseum |
| National Petroleum Corporation of Namibia (NAMCOR) | Namibische Mineralölgesellschaft |
| National Planning Commission | Nationale Planungskommission |
| National Road Safety Council (NRSC) | Nationaler Verkehrssicherheitsrat |
| National Union of Namibian Workers | Gewerkschaftsdachverband Namibias |

## O

| | |
|---|---|
| Office of the President | Präsidialamt |
| Office of the Prime Minister | Amt des Premierministers (der Premierministerin) |

## P

| | |
|---|---|
| Parliamentary Standing Committee on Public Accounts | Ständiger Parlamentsausschuss für öffentliche Ausgaben/Bilanzen |
| Permanent Secretary | Staatssekretär(in) |

| | |
|---|---|
| permit | Permit, Erlaubnisschein, Erlaubnis, Genehmigung |
| policy | Politik, Richtlinie, Strategie, Programm |
| policy framework | Rahmenrichtlinien, -bedingungen |
| policy planning | Richtlinienplanung, Strategieplanung |
| primary health care | medizinische Grundversorgung |
| prime lending rate | Leitzins, Leitzinssatz |
| Public Service Commission (PSC) | Kommission für den öffentlichen Dienst |
| Public Service Union of Namibia (PSUN) | Namibische Dienstleistungsgewerkschaft |

## R

| | |
|---|---|
| Regional Council | Regionalrat |
| reproductive health | reproduktive Gesundheit |
| Road Fund Administration (RFA) | Straßenbaufonds |
| Roads Authority | Straßenbaubehörde |
| Roads Contractor Company (RCC) | Straßenbauunternehmen, -firma |

## S

| | |
|---|---|
| Southern African Customs Union (SACU) | Zollunion Südliches Afrika (ZUSA) |
| SACU Revenue Pool | Einnahmekartell der Zollunion Südliches Afrika |
| Southern African Development Community (SADC) | Entwicklungsgemeinschaft Südliches Afrika (ESA) |
| Social Security Commission (SSC) | Sozialversicherung |
| Southern African Power Pool (SAPP) | Energieversorgungskartell Südliches Afrika |
| Speaker of Parliament | Parlamentspräsident(in), Speaker des Parlaments |
| State Owned Enterprises Governing Council Secretariat | Sekretariat des Aufsichtsrates für Staatsunternehmen |

## T

| | |
|---|---|
| tender | Tender, Ausschreibung |
| Tender Board | Vergabebehörde, Zentrale Vergabestelle |
| Tour and Safari Association of Namibia (TASA) | Namibischer Tour- und Safariunternehmerverband |
| Tourism Expo | Touristikmesse |
| traditional laws and practices | Stammesgesetze und Gebräuche, Gewohnheitsrecht |

## U

| | |
|---|---|
| Undersecretary | Unterstaatssekretär(in) |

## V

| | |
|---|---|
| valuation roll | Abschätzungsverzeichnis |
| value-added tax | Mehrwertsteuer |
| value adding | Wertschöpfung |
| Vocational Training Centre | Berufsbildungszentrum, (Handwerkliche) Berufsschule |

## W

| | |
|---|---|
| wild cat strike | Ausstand |
| workshop | Arbeitstagung, Arbeitsgruppe, Workshop |

# Law and Related Matters

# Rechtswesen

## A

| | |
|---|---|
| acting judge | amtierende(r), stellvertretende(r) Richter(in) |
| advocate | Rechtsanwalt (-anwältin), Advokat(in) *(höhere Stellung als Rechtsanwalt, richtet sich nach Streitwert)* |
| amend (to) | novellieren |
| amendment of law | Novelle, Revision, Änderung des Gesetzes |
| annual leave | Jahresurlaub |
| appeal hearing | Berufungsverfahren, Revisionsverfahren |
| arbitration | Schlichtung(-sverfahren) |
| Attorney General | Generalstaatsanwalt (-anwältin) |

## B

| | |
|---|---|
| barrister | Rechtsanwalt (-anwältin) *(in niedrigerer Stellung als Advokat(in))* |
| basic working conditions | Arbeitsbedingungen |

## C

| | |
|---|---|
| certificates of employment | Arbeitsbescheinigung, Arbeitsnachweis |
| Chief Justice | Oberrichter |
| code of good practice | faire Verfahrensregeln |
| compassionate leave | Sonderurlaub aufgrund eines Todes-/Trauerfalls |
| conciliation | Schlichtung |
| customary law reform | Gewohnheitsrechtreform |

## D

| | |
|---|---|
| defence | Verteidigung |
| disciplinary hearing | Disziplinarverfahren |
| dispute | Disput, Kontroverse |

## E

| | |
|---|---|
| evidence | Beweis, Beweismittel |
| extended maternity leave | verlängerter Mutterschaftsurlaub/ Erziehungsurlaub |

## F

| | |
|---|---|
| freedom of assembly | Versammlungsfreiheit |
| freedom of association | Vereinigungsfreiheit, Koalitionsfreiheit |
| fundamental rights and protections | Grundrechte |

## G

| | |
|---|---|
| Government Gazette | Staatsanzeiger, Amtsblatt |

## H

| | |
|---|---|
| high court | Obergericht |

## I

| | |
|---|---|
| instruments of law | juristische Handhabung, Rechtsmittel |

## J

| | |
|---|---|
| judge | Richter(in) |
| judgement | Urteil, Rechtsspruch, |
| Judge President | Gerichtspräsident(in) |
| jurisdiction and powers of court | Zuständigkeit und Machtbefugnis des Gerichts |

## L

| | |
|---|---|
| labour court | Arbeitsgericht |
| Law Reform and Development Commission | Rechtsreform/Gesetzesreform und Entwicklungsausschuss |
| lawyer | Anwalt (Anwältin), Jurist(in) |
| Legal Assistance Centre (LAC) | Rechtsbeistandszentrum, Rechtshilfezentrum |
| leave of absence | Beurlaubung |
| liability | Haftung, Haftpflicht, Haftbarkeit, Verbindlichkeit |
| lock-out | Aussperrung |
| lower court | Vorinstanz |

## M

| | |
|---|---|
| magistrate | Magistrat(in), Amtsrichter(in) |
| magistrate's court | Magistratsgericht |

## N

| | |
|---|---|
| night work | Nachtarbeit |
| night shift | Nachtschicht |

## O

| | |
|---|---|
| Office of the Prime Minister | Amt/Büro des Premierministers (der Premierministerin) |

## P

| | |
|---|---|
| paralegal | Rechtsassistent(in) ohne formaljuristische Ausbildung |
| pending dispute | anhängiger Streitgegenstand |
| period of employment | Dauer des Angestelltenverhältnisses |
| prevention and resolution of disputes | Konfliktbeilegung |
| Promulgation of Act of Parliament | Verkündung eines (vom Parlament verabschiedeten) Gesetzes |

| | |
|---|---|
| prosecution | strafrechtliche Verfolgung |
| prosecutor | Ankläger(in) |
| Prosecutor General | Staatsankläger(in), Generalstaatsanwalt (-anwältin) |
| provisions of act | gesetzliche Vorschrift |

## R

| | |
|---|---|
| remuneration | Bezahlung, Vergütung |
| repeal of law | Aufhebung/Widerrufung des Gesetzes |
| resolution of transitional matters | Übergangslösung |

## S

| | |
|---|---|
| salary | Gehalt |
| severance pay | Abfindung, Entlassungsabfindung |
| sick leave | Krankheitsurlaub, Krankschreibung |
| supreme court | Verfassungsgericht, Oberster Gerichtshof |

## T

| | |
|---|---|
| termination of employment on notice | Beendigung des Arbeitsverhältnisses durch Kündigung |
| trade union | Gewerkschaft |

## W

| | |
|---|---|
| wage commission | Tarifkommission |
| wage order | Tariffestsetzung |
| wage negotiation | Lohnverhandlung, Tarifverhandlung |
| wage policy | Lohnpolitik |
| wage demand | Lohnforderung |
| wage increase | Lohnerhöhung |

# Special Education | Sonderpädagogik

## A

| | |
|---|---|
| acoustician | Akustiker(in) |
| Additional Educational Needs (AEN) | pädagogischer Förderbedarf |
| aphasia | Aphasie *(eine Form der Sprachstörung)* |
| assistive devices | technische Hilfen und Geräte |
| audiogram | Audiogramm |
| audiology | Audiologie |
| audiologist | Audiologe (Audiologin) *(in Deutschland spezialisierte Fachärzte, im südlichen Afrika „paramedical professionals")* |
| audiometer | Audiometer *(Gerät zur Messung des Hörvermögens)* |
|   - screening audiometer |   - für Aussonderungsuntersuchungen |
|   - diagnostic audiometer |   - zur Messung von Luft- und Knochenleitung |
| auditory perception | auditive Wahrnehmung |
| auditory perception problem | auditive Wahrnehmungsstörung |
| autism | Autismus |
| autistic | autistisch, ein Mensch mit Autismus |

## B

| | |
|---|---|
| behavioural difficulty | Verhaltensauffälligkeit, Verhaltensstörung |
| big/enlarged print | Großdruck |
| Braille | Blindenschrift |

## C

| | |
|---|---|
| cerebral palsy (CP) | Zerebralparese |
| CHAIN (Children with Handicaps – Action in Namibia) | Hilfsorganisation für Kinder mit Behinderungen |

| | |
|---|---|
| CLaSH (The Association for Children with Language, Speech and Hearing Impairments of Namibia) | Hilfsorganisation für Kinder mit Hör-, Sprach- und Sprechstörungen |
| cochlear implant (CI) | Cochlea Implantat (CI) |
| congenital | angeboren |

## D

| | |
|---|---|
| deaf | gehörlos, taub |
| deaf blind | taubblind |
| disability | Funktionsstörung, Funktionsbeeinträchtigung |
| disability issues | Behindertenfragen |
| disabled | behindert |
| disadvantaged<br>- culturally<br>- educationally<br>- socially | benachteiligt<br>- in kultureller Hinsicht<br>- in pädagogischer Hinsicht<br>- in sozialer Hinsicht |
| disorder | Störung |
| Division: Diagnostic, Advisory and Training Services | Abteilung des Erziehungsministeriums, die sich mit Diagnostik, Beratung und Fortbildung befasst |
| Division: Special Programmes and Schools | Abteilung des Erziehungsministeriums, die sich mit Sonderpädagogik befasst |
| Down syndrome | Down-Syndrom |
| dyscalculia | Dyskalkulie, Rechenschwäche |
| dyslexia | Legasthenie, Lese-Rechtschreibschwäche |
| dyslexic (he/she is dyslexic) | er/sie ist Legastheniker(in) |

## E

| | |
|---|---|
| early childhood development (ECD) | frühkindliche Entwicklung |
| educationally marginalised children | vom Bildungssystem vernachlässigte Kinder |
| emotional difficulty | emotionale Störung, Störung des Gefühlslebens |
| ENT (Ear, Nose and Throat) | HNO (Hals-Nasen-Ohren) |

## G

| | |
|---|---|
| gifted | hochbegabt |
| grass roots | Basis |
| grass root level | Basisebene, Basisansatz |
| grommets | Paukenröhrchen |

## H

| | |
|---|---|
| handicap (social) | Beeinträchtigung, Behinderung (soziale) |
| handicapped | behindert |
| hard-of-hearing | schwerhörig |
| health professionals | im Gesundheitswesen Tätige |
| hearing aid<br>- behind-the-ear aid<br>- in-the-ear aid<br>- pocket aid | Hörgerät<br>- Hinter-dem-Ohr-Gerät<br>- Im-Ohr-Gerät<br>- Taschengerät |
| hearing impaired | hörgeschädigt |
| hearing loss<br>- mild<br>- moderate<br>- severe<br>- profound | Hörverlust<br>- leicht<br>- mittelgradig<br>- hochgradig<br>- total |
| sudden hearing loss | Hörsturz |
| hemiplegic | halbseitig/einseitig gelähmt |

## I

| | |
|---|---|
| impairment<br>- mental<br>- visual<br><br>- hearing<br><br>- physical<br>- sensory<br>- speech, language | Schädigung<br>- geistige Behinderung<br>- Sehschädigung, Blindheit, Sehbehinderung<br>- Hörschädigung (Gehörlosigkeit, Schwerhörigkeit)<br>- Körperbehinderung<br>- Sinnesschädigung<br>- Sprech-, Sprachbehinderung |

| | |
|---|---|
| Inclusive Education (IE) | Inklusive Pädagogik |
| integration | integrativer Unterricht |

## L

| | |
|---|---|
| language delay | Sprachentwicklungsverzögerung |
| language development | Sprachentwicklung |
| language stimulation | Sprachstimulation, Sprachanbahnung |
| learning difficulty | Lernschwäche |
| learning disability | Lernstörung, Lernbehinderung |
| literacy | Schreib- und Lesefähigkeit, Alphabetisierung |
| literacy programme | Alphabetisierungskampagne |

## M

| | |
|---|---|
| mainstream | allgemeines Schulsystem, Regelschulwesen |
| meningitis | Hirnhautentzündung, Meningitis |
| mentally challenged | geistig behindert |
| middle ear infection (= otitis media) | Mittelohrentzündung |
| multiple disabilities | Mehrfachbehinderung |
| muscle tone | Muskeltonus, Spannungszustand des Muskels |
| - low | - herabgesetzte Muskelspannung (hypoton) |
| - high | - übersteigerte Muskelspannung (hyperton) |

## N

| | |
|---|---|
| Namibia National Association of the Deaf (NNAD) | Namibische Vereinigung der Gehörlosen, Namibischer Gehörlosenverein |
| Namibian Sign Language (NSL) | Namibische Gebärdensprache |
| National Federation of People with Disabilities in Namibia (NFPDN) | Dachorganisation der Behinderten/ behinderter Menschen in Namibia |

| | |
|---|---|
| National Federation of the Visually Impaired (NFVI) | Dachorganisation der Sehbehinderten |
| National Institute for Special Education (NISE) | Staatliches Institut für Sonderpädagogik |
| numeracy | Rechenfähigkeit, mathematische Fähigkeit |

## O

| | |
|---|---|
| occupational therapist (OT) | Arbeits-, Ergo-, Beschäftigungstherapeut(in) |
| organisation of persons with disabilities | Behindertenorganisation |
| Orphans and Vulnerable Children (OVC) | Waisen und schutzbedürftige Kinder |
| outcome oriented | ergebnisorientiert |

## P

| | |
|---|---|
| paramedical | paramedizinisch, den medizinischen Berufen zugehörig |
| paramedic | Sanitäter(in) |
| paraplegic | beidseitig/doppelseitig gelähmt |
| performance-based | leistungsabhängig |
| peripatetic teacher | Kooperationslehrer(in), Betreuungslehrer(in) *(für mehrere Schulen zuständig)* |
| persons with disabilities | Behinderte |
| physically disabled | körperbehindert |
| physiotherapist | Krankengymnast(in), Physiotherapeut(in) |
| policy on people with disabilities | Richtlinie für den Umgang mit Menschen mit Behinderung |
| prosthesis | Prothese |

## R

| | |
|---|---|
| Regional School Counsellor (RSC) | pädagogische(r) und psychologische(r) Berater(in) für Lerner(innen)/ Schüler(innen) |

## S

| | |
|---|---|
| sensorineural hearing loss | Innenohrschaden |
| sensory integration problem | Wahrnehmungsstörung |
| sheltered employment | geschützte Beschäftigung, unterstützte Arbeitsplätze |
| sheltered workshop | geschützte/beschützende Werkstätte |
| sign language interpreter | Gebärdensprachdolmetscher(in) |
| special educational needs (SEN) | sonderpädagogische Bedürfnisse |
| special needs | besondere Bedürfnisse |
| special school | Sonderschule, Förderschule |
| speech discrimination test | Sprachaudiogramm (Messung der Sprachwahrnehmung) |
| speech therapy | Sprachtherapie |
| speech and language therapist (SLT) | Sprachtherapeut(in), Logopäde (Logopädin) |
| stammer (to) | stottern, stockendes Sprechen |
| stutter (to) | stottern, stockendes Sprechen |

## V

| | |
|---|---|
| visual perception | visuelle Wahrnehmung |

## W

| | |
|---|---|
| wheelchair user | Rollstuhlfahrer(in) |

# Gender Issues | Geschlechterfragen

## A

| | |
|---|---|
| Affirmative Action (Employment) Act of 1998 | Gesetz zur Gleichstellung am Arbeitsplatz |
| African Charter on Human and People's Rights | Afrikanische Charta der Menschenrechte |
| AIDS pandemic | AIDS Pandemie |
| All Africa Rights Initiative | Afrikanische Rechtsinitiative |
| anti-retroviral drugs (ARV) | antiretrovirale Medikamente |
| Association for Progressive Communications Women's Networking Support Programme (APC WNSP) | Internationales Netzwerk für soziale Gerechtigkeit, Frieden, Umweltschutz, Menschenrechte durch die Bereitstellung von Kommunikations-Infrastruktur |
| AU Protocol on the Rights of Women in Africa | AU-Protokoll zu Frauenrechten in Afrika |

## B

| | |
|---|---|
| Bill on Gay Marriages | Gesetzesentwurf zur homosexuellen Eheschließung |
| bride price, lobola | Brautpreis |
| brotherhood | Bruderschaft, Brüderlichkeit |

## C

| | |
|---|---|
| Child Care and Protection Act | Kinderbetreuungs- und Kinderschutzgesetz |
| child marriage | Kinderehe, Kindweibehe |
| Children's Status Bill | Gesetzesentwurf zur Rechtsstellung von Kindern |
| civil enforcement efforts | zivilrechtliche Durchsetzungsanstrengung |
| Combating of Rape Act | Gesetz zur Vergewaltigungsbekämpfung |

| | |
|---|---|
| Convention on the Elimination of All Forms of Discrimination Against Women (CEDAW) | Kongress zur Beseitigung aller Diskriminierung von Frauen |
| Criminal Procedure and Amendment Act | Strafverfahren und Änderungsgesetz |
| cultural practices | kulturelle Bräuche, kulturabhängige Gewohnheiten |
| customary marriage | Stammesehe |

## D

| | |
|---|---|
| different forms of co-habitation | unterschiedliche Formen des Zusammenlebens |
| diverse sexual orientations | verschiedene/unterschiedliche sexuelle Veranlagungen |
| Divorce Act | Scheidungsgesetz |
| Domestic Violence Act | Gesetz zur Bekämpfung häuslicher Gewalt |
| dowry crimes | Mitgiftverbrechen |
| drop-in centre | Anlaufstelle |

## E

| | |
|---|---|
| Employment Equity Commission | Kommission zur Gleichstellung am Arbeitsplatz |
| equal sharing of domestic responsibilities | ausgewogene Verteilung der Haushaltspflichten |

## F

| | |
|---|---|
| female genital mutilation | weibliche Genitalverstümmelung |

## G

| | |
|---|---|
| Gender and Media (GEM) | Geschlechter und Medien |
| Gender and Media Southern Africa Network (GEMSA) | Geschlechter und Medien Netzwerk Südliches Afrika |
| gender balance of appointments | ausgewogenes Geschlechterverhältnis bei Anstellungen |

| | |
|---|---|
| gender based violence | geschlechterbezogene/ geschlechtsspezifische Gewalt |
| gender budgeting | Gleichstellungsetat |
| gender desk | Dienststelle für Gleichstellungsfragen |
| gender dynamics | Geschlechterdynamik |
| gender equality | Geschlechtergleichheit, Gleichstellung von Frauen und Männern |
| gender justification | Gleichstellungsrechtfertigung |
| gender mainstreaming | durchgängige Gleichstellungsorientierung |
| gender policies | Gleichstellungspolitik, Richtlinien der Geschlechter |
| Gender Research and Advocacy Project | Geschlechterforschungs- und Förderungsprojekt |
| gender sensitivity training | Gleichstellungssensibilitätstraining |
| gender-related legislation | gleichstellungsbezogene Gesetzgebung |
| global inequality | globale Ungleichheit |
| good governance | verantwortungsbewusste/gute Regierungsführung |
| grass roots women's network | Frauennetzwerk an der Basis, Frauen-Netzwerk auf Basisebene |

## H

| | |
|---|---|
| human trafficking | Menschenhandel |

## I

| | |
|---|---|
| International Gay and Lesbian Human Rights Movement | Internationale Menschenrechtsbewegung der Schwulen und Lesben |

## J

| | |
|---|---|
| joint custody and equal guardianship | gemeinsames Sorgerecht und gleichberechtigte Vormundschaft |

## M

| | |
|---|---|
| Maintenance Act | Gesetz zur Unterhaltszahlung |
| maintenance investigators | Unterhaltsermittler |
| male worshipping | Vergötterung des männlichen Geschlechts, Männerverehrung |
| Married Persons Equality Act 1 of 1996 | Ehegatten-Gleichstellungsgesetz |

## N

| | |
|---|---|
| Namibia Planned Parenthood Association (NAPPA) | Namibischer Verein für Familienplanung |
| Namibian Demographic and Health Survey | Namibische Demographie- und Gesundheitsumfrage |
| Namibian Women's Manifesto Network | Namibisches Frauenmanifest-Netzwerk |
| National Executive Committee of the Namibian NGO Forum (NANGOF Trust) Gender Sector | Nationaler Exekutivausschuss des Namibischen NGO Forums (NANGOF) für Geschlechterfragen |

## P

| | |
|---|---|
| post-exposure prophylaxis to reduce chances of HIV-infection (PEP) | Postexpositionsprophylaxe zur Verhütung einer HIV-Infektion |
| polygamy | Polygamie, Mehrehe, Vielweiberei |
| Prevention of Parent to Child Transmission Programme (of HIV) | Programm zur Verhütung der HIV-Übertragung von Eltern auf Kinder |
| promote women's participation (to) | die Teilnahme von Frauen an Entscheidungsprozessen fördern |
| property grabbing from widows | Eigentumsklau von Witwen |
| Proportional Representation (PR) System (in legislation, local elections) | Verhältniswahlsystem, Verhältniswahl (in der Gesetzgebung und bei Gemeindewahlen) |

## R

| | |
|---|---|
| Recognition of Customary Marriage Bill | Gesetzesentwurf zur Anerkennung von Stammesehen |

| | |
|---|---|
| rights of girls and women | Rechte von Mädchen und Frauen |
| rights of sexual minorities | Rechte sexueller Minderheiten |
| rights-awareness organisations | Bürgerrechtsorganisationen |

## S

| | |
|---|---|
| SADC Protocol and Declaration on Gender and Development | SADC-Erklärung zur Geschlechter- und Entwicklungspolitik |
| same sex marriage | gleichgeschlechtliche Ehe, Homoehe |
| sex trafficking of women and girls | Sextourismus, Sexualhandel mit Frauen und Mädchen |
| sexual advantage (to take) | sexuell ausnutzen, belästigen |
| sexual and reproductive rights | sexuelle und fortpflanzungsbezogene Rechte |
| sisterhood | Schwesternschaft (Nonnen), Schwesterlichkeit |
| Southern Africa Gender Justice Barometer | Gleichstellungsbarometer im Südlichen Afrika |
| social cohesion deficit | soziales Zusammenhaltsdefizit, Fehlen sozialen Zusammenhalts |

## T

| | |
|---|---|
| transgender people | Transsexuelle |

## U

| | |
|---|---|
| University of Namibia's Gender Training and Research Programme | Gleichstellungsschulungs- und Forschungsprogramm der Universität Namibia |
| unsupportive parents | unkooperative Eltern |

## V

| | |
|---|---|
| Victim Support Programme | Programm zur Opferbetreuung |
| violations of women's sexual rights | Verletzung der sexuellen Rechte der Frauen |
| vulnerable witnesses | verletzliche Zeugen |

## W

| | |
|---|---|
| widow immolation | Witwenopferung, Witwenverbrennung |
| Women and Child Protection Unit | Einheit zum Schutz von Frauen und Kindern |
| women's empowerment | Frauenförderung, Selbstbestimmung der Frauen |
| women's human rights | Menschenrechte der Frauen |
| women's political and economic empowerment | politische und wirtschaftliche Handlungsfähigkeit der Frauen |
| women's solidarity | Solidarität von Frauen, Frauensolidarität |

# Deutsch-Englisch

# Schule und Schulverwaltung | Schools and Administration

## A

| | |
|---|---|
| Abschlussprüfung | final examination |
| abgelehnt (Zulassung) | (admission) refused |
| Absolvent(in) | graduate |
| Abteilungsleiter(in) | head of department (primary, secondary school) |
| akademische Bildung | higher education, university education |
| akademischer Fortschritt | academic progress |
| Allgemeinbildung | general education |
| allgemeine Verhaltensregeln | general rules of behaviour, conduct |
| Alphabetisierungskampagne | literacy campaign |
| Altschüler(innen) | alumni, former students |
| Alumni, Alumnus, Alumna | alumni, alumnus, alumna |
| Anmeldebestimmungen | conditions of registration |
| Anmeldeformular | application form |
| Anmeldung | enrolment, registration |
| Anmerkungen des Prüfers (der Prüferin) | marker's comments |
| Anpassung der Noten (an die Gaußsche Normalverteilungskurve) | grade review |
| Ansatz | approach |
| Antrag | application |
| Anwesenheit (Schule) | school attendance |
| Arbeitsgemeinschaft (AG) | extra-curricular activity |
| Attest | certificate |
| Aufgabenblatt | question paper, examination paper, work sheet |
| Aufnahme von Lernenden ungeachtet der Rasse, Hautfarbe, ethnischer oder konfessioneller Zugehörigkeit | admission of learners not based on race, ethnic origin or colour and creed |

| | |
|---|---|
| Aufnahmeantrag | application for admission |
| Aufnahmebedingungen | terms and conditions of admission |
| Aufnahmeprüfung | access test, entrance exam |
| Aufsichtsgremium einer Schule | controlling body of a school |
| Aufsichtsrat | supervisory council |
| Ausbildung | education, training |
| Auslandsdienstlehrkraft (ADLK) | seconded teacher, teacher abroad |
| Ausschluss eines Lernenden (einer Lernenden) vom Unterricht | suspension of a learner |
| Ausschuss | committee |
| außerhalb des Lehr-, Stundenplans | extracurricular |
| außerschulisch | extracurricular |
| außerschulische Veranstaltung | extracurricular activity |
| Ausstattung mit Unterrichtsmaterial | provision of teaching materials |
| auswerten | evaluate (to) |
| Auswertung | evaluation |

## B

| | |
|---|---|
| Basislehrplan | core curriculum |
| Beamter (Beamtin) des Bildungsministeriums | education officer |
| befähigen | empower (to) |
| Befähigung zur Leistungseinschätzung | (assessing) competence |
| befugt sein zu | to be authorized to, to be empowered to |
| Begegnungsschule | contact school |
| Beitrag der Eltern | contribution by parents |
| benoten | grade (to) |
| beratendes Gremium | advisory council/committee |
| Beratungsausschuss | advisory council/committee |
| berufsbegleitende Lehrfortbildung | in-service-teacher training |
| Berufsberatung | career guidance |
| Berufserfahrung | work experience |

| | |
|---|---|
| Berufsrichtlinien für Lehrer(innen), Lehrende | professional standards for teachers |
| Bescheinigung | certificate |
| beschlussfähig sein (Versammlung) | constitute a quorum (to) |
| bestätigen | verify (to), moderate (to) |
| beurteilen | evaluate (to) |
| Beurteilung | assessment, evaluation |
| Beurteilungsbogen | assessment form |
| Beurteilungsformular | assessment form |
| Bewerbung | application |
| bewerten | evaluate (to) |
| Bewertung | assessment, valuation, evaluation |
| Bewertungsmatrix | marking scheme |
| Bewertungsschema | marking scheme |
| Bildung | education |
| Bildungsanstalt | educational establishment/institution |
| Bildungschancen | educational opportunities |
| Bildungseinrichtung | educational establishment/institution |
| Bildungskrise | education crisis |
| Bildungsministerium | Ministry of Education |
| Bildungsniveau | educational level |
| Bildungsnotstand | education crisis |
| Bildungspolitik | education policy, educational policy |
| Bildungsreform | educational reform |
| Bildungsrichtlinien | education policy, educational policy |
| Bildungsstand | educational level |
| Bildungsstätte | educational establishment/institution |
| Bildungsstufe | educational level |
| Bildungssystem | education system |
| Bundesprogrammlehrkraft (BPLK) | Federal Programme Teacher, seconded teacher |
| Bundesverwaltungsamt | Federal Office of Administration |

Schule und Schulverwaltung | Schools and Administration

| | |
|---|---|
| Büro des Schulleiters (der Schulleiterin) | principal's office |

## C

| | |
|---|---|
| Curriculum | curriculum |

## D

| | |
|---|---|
| Deutscher Fachunterricht (DFU) | Content and Language Integrated Learning in German (CLIL) |
| Deutsches Sprachdiplom | German Language Diploma |
| Dienstleistungsbetrieb | service company |
| Diplom | diploma, degree |
| Disziplinarkonferenz | disciplinary conference |
| Disziplinarverfahren | disciplinary hearing |
| dokumentarischer Nachweis | documentary evidence |
| Dozent(in) | lecturer |
| Dyskalkulie | dyscalculia |

## E

| | |
|---|---|
| Eigenverantwortliches Arbeiten (EVA) | self-responsible learning, learning independently |
| Eignungstest (Universität) | aptitude test |
| Einführung | introduction, approach |
| Einschätzung | evaluation |
| Einschreibung | registration, enrolment |
| Einschulungstest | school readiness test |
| Einstufung der Staatsschulen und Heime | classification of state schools and hostels |
| Elternabend | parents evening |
| Elternanteil | contribution by parents |
| Elternbeirat | parents representative council |
| Elternversammlung | parents meeting |
| Elternvertreter(in) | parents representative |
| englischsprachiger Zweig | English medium branch |

| | |
|---|---|
| Erfahrung im Unterrichten | teaching practice |
| ermächtigen | empower (to) |
| Erwachsenenbildung | adult education |
| Erwartungshorizont | marking scheme |
| Erziehung | education |
| Erziehungssystem | education system |
| Erziehungstheorie | educational theory |
| Evaluation | evaluation |
| Examen | exam, examination |
| Examensausschuss | examining body |
| Examensbogen | question paper, examination paper |
| Examinator(in) | examiner |

## F

| | |
|---|---|
| Fach | subject |
| Fachdidaktik | subject methodology and didactics |
| Fachhochschulreife | advanced technical certificate, exemption for universities of applied sciences |
| Fachkonferenz | subject meeting |
| Fachlehrplan | syllabus, curriculum |
| Fachmethodik | subject methodology and didactics |
| Fachrichtung (bestimmte) | special course of study |
| Fachstudium | professional studies |
| Fachunterricht | subject teaching |
| Fehlverhalten | misconduct |
| Feinmotorik | fine motor skills |
| Fernstudium | distance education |
| Finanzverwalter(in) | Bursar (UNAM) |
| Förderkonzept für die Primarstufe | concept of support for primary grades |
| Förderkonzept für die Sekundarstufe I | concept of support for junior secondary grades |

| | |
|---|---|
| Förderrahmen (finanziell) | criteria of support |
| Förderschule | special school |
| Förderung von Lernenden | learner support |
| Förderunterricht | remedial teaching/education |
| formloses Lernen | informal learning |
| Formular ausfüllen | fill in a form (to) |
| Fragebogen | question paper, examination paper |
| Freiarbeit | open learning |

## G

| | |
|---|---|
| Gebührenbefreiung | exemption from payment |
| gegenlesen | moderate (to) |
| gemeinsamer Unterricht von Jungen und Mädchen | coeducation |
| Gesamtkonferenz (GLK) | staff meeting |
| Gesamtlehrerkonferenz | staff meeting |
| graduieren | graduate (to) |
| Graduierte(r) | graduate |
| Gremium | committee, board |
| Grobmotorik | gross motor skills |
| Grundschulausbildung | primary education |
| Grundschule | primary school |

## H

| | |
|---|---|
| Haftungsausschlussformular | indemnity form |
| handelnd lernen | learning by doing |
| Hauptprüfungsbeauftragte(r) | chief examiner |
| Hausordnung | house rules |
| Hausunterricht | home schooling |
| Heimausschuss | hostel committee |
| Heimelternvertretung | hostel parents' representative council |
| Heimgebühren | boarding fees |

| | |
|---|---|
| Heimleitung | hostel management |
| heimlicher Lehrplan | hidden curriculum |
| Hochschulbildung | tertiary education, higher education, university education |
| Hochschullehrende | lecturer |
| Hochschulzugangsberechtigung | university exemption |
| Home Schooling | home schooling |
| hospitieren | sit in (to) |

## I

| | |
|---|---|
| Informatik | computer science |
| Immatrikulation | registration |
| Immatrikulationsberechtigung | matriculation exemption *(to have the right to enrol at a university)* |
| informelles Lernen | informal learning |
| inklusive Pädagogik | inclusive education |
| institutionelle Rahmenbedingungen | institutional framework requirements |
| integrative Erziehung | inclusive education |
| Internat | hostel |

## K

| | |
|---|---|
| Klasse | grade |
| Kernlehrplan | core curriculum |
| Klassenarbeit | class test |
| Klassenausflug | class outing |
| Klassenfahrt | class outing |
| Klassenunterricht | class teaching |
| Klausur | exam, examination, test |
| Koedukation | coeducation |
| Kollegium | staff (members) |
| Komitee | committee |
| Konferenz | conference |

| | |
|---|---|
| Konrektor(in) | Pro-Vice-Chancellor |
| körperliche Züchtigung | corporal punishment |
| Korrekturlesen (der Prüfungsbögen/ Prüfungsarbeiten) | proofreading (of examination papers/ scripts) |
| korrigieren | correct (to), mark (to) |
| kostenlose, kostenfreie Lernmittel | free learning aids |
| Krabbelgruppe | toddlers group |
| Kulturreferent(in) (Botschaft) | Head of Cultural Affairs/Cultural Desk |
| Kultusministerkonferenz (KMK) | Standing Conference of the Ministers of Education and Cultural Affairs of the Länder (federal states) in the Federal Republic of Germany |
| Kurztest | short test |

## L

| | |
|---|---|
| Learning by Doing | learning by doing |
| Legasthenie | dyslexia |
| Lehr- und Lerntheorie | educational theory |
| Lehramtsanwärter(in) | student teacher |
| Lehrbefähigung | teaching competency |
| Lehrende(r) | teacher |
| Lehrer(in) | teacher |
| Lehrerbeirat | teachers representative committee, teachers advisory board |
| Lehrergewerkschaft Namibias | Teachers Union of Namibia (TUN) |
| Lehrerzimmer | staff room |
| Lehrkompetenz | teaching competency |
| Lehrmethode | teaching method |
| Lehrmittel | teaching aids |
| Lehrmittelbereitstellung | provision of teaching materials |
| Lehrmittelzentrum | teachers resource centre |
| Lehrplan | syllabus, curriculum |
| Lehrplanentwicklung | curriculum development |

| | |
|---|---|
| Leistungseinschätzung | (performance) assessment |
| Leitbild | mission statement |
| Leiter(in) der Kulturabteilung | Head of Cultural Affairs/Cultural Desk |
| Lenkungsausschuss | steering committee |
| Lern- und Lehrmittel | learning and teaching aids |
| lernbehindert | learning-disabled, slow learner |
| Lernende(r) | student, learner |
| Lerner(in) | learner, student |
| Lernerfolg | learning achievement |
| Lernerfolgskontrolle | learning evaluation |
| Lerninhalte | learning content |
| Lernmethode | learning method |
| Lernmittelfreiheit | free learning aids |
| Lernprozess | learning process |
| Lernstörung | learning disability |
| Lerntypen | learning types |
| Lernziele | (learning) aims and objectives |
| Lese- und Rechtschreibschwäche | dyslexia |

## M

| | |
|---|---|
| Medien im Unterricht | media in teaching |
| Mediathek | teachers resource centre, media centre |
| Mentor | mentor |
| Methodenvielfalt | variety of teaching methods |
| Methodenwechsel (didaktischer) | change of teaching methods |
| Methodik | methodology |
| Mindestanforderungen | minimum requirements |
| Mindestniveau | minimum standards |
| Mindestnorm | minimum standards |
| Mindeststandard | minimum standards |
| Modul | module |

| | |
|---|---|
| Multiplatz | multi-purpose sports field |
| mündliche Prüfung | oral examination |

## N

| | |
|---|---|
| Nachhilfeunterricht | extra lessons |
| Namibische Nationale Lehrergewerkschaft | Namibian National Teachers Union (NANTU) |
| Neue Primarstufe | New Primary School |
| Neue Sekundarstufe | English Medium Branch |
| Note | mark, grade |
| Noteneinstufung | grade rating |
| Notenschwellenwert | grade threshold |
| NSSC-Abschluss | Namibia Senior Secondary Certificate (NSSC) *(university entrance diploma)* |

## O

| | |
|---|---|
| Oberstufe(-nschule) | secondary school |
| Offener Unterricht (OU) | open learning |
| Ortslehrkraft | local teacher |

## P

| | |
|---|---|
| Pädagogischer Beirat | pedagogical/educational advisory board |
| Pädagogik | educational theory, theory of education, education |
| Personalangelegenheiten | staff matters |
| Personalfragen | staff matters |
| Polytechnikum Namibia | Polytechnic of Namibia (PON) |
| Praktikant(in) | intern |
| Praktikum | internship |
| praktischer Unterricht | practical teaching |
| praktisches Lernen | learning by doing |
| Preis-Leistungs-Verhältnis | price-performance ratio |

| | |
|---|---|
| Primarstufenbildung | primary education |
| Privatschule | private school |
| Privatstunden | private lessons/tuition |
| Privatunterricht | private lessons/tuition |
| Programm zur Verbesserung des Schul- und Ausbildungsbereichs | Education and Training Sector Improvement Programme (ETSIP) |
| Projektarbeit | project work |
| Prorektor(in) | Pro-Vice-Chancellor |
| Protokollführer(in) | secretary |
| Prüfer(in) | examiner |
| Prüfung | exam, examination, test |
| Prüfungsausschuss | board of examiners, examining body |
| Prüfungsbogen | question paper, examination paper |
| Prüfungsentwurf | draft examination paper |
| Prüfungsordnung | examination regulations |
| Prüfungsvorschlag | draft examination paper |
| Prügelstrafe | corporal punishment |

## R

| | |
|---|---|
| ReFo (Regionale Fortbildung) | Regional Training Course |
| Rechenschwäche | dyscalculia |
| Referendar(in) | student teacher |
| Referendariat | internship |
| Regierungsschule | state school, government school |
| Regionaler Erziehungsausschuss | Regional Education Forum |
| Regionales Bildungsforum | Regional Education Forum |
| Registrar(in) | Registrar |
| Registrator(in) | Registrar |
| Registrierung | registration |
| Rektor(in) | Vice-Chancellor |

## S

| | |
|---|---|
| Schilf (Schulinterne Lehrerfortbildung) | school-based training for teachers |
| schriftliche Prüfung | written examination |
| schriftliche Zusage | letter of acceptance |
| schriftlicher Verweis | notice of warning |
| Schulaufsichtsgremium | controlling body of a school |
| Schulausschluss | expulsion/suspension of a learner |
| Schulbeihilfe | school subsidy |
| Schulbeihilfe aus öffentlichen Geldern | subsidy of schools |
| Schuldirektor(in) | headmaster, headmistress, principal |
| Schule mit Primar- und Sekundarstufe | combined school |
| Schule mit Schülerheim | boarding school |
| Schulentwicklung | school development |
| Schulentwicklungsfonds | school development fund |
| Schüler(in) | learner |
| Schülerheim | hostel |
| Schülermitverantwortung (SMV) | Learners' Representative Council |
| Schülermitverwaltung | learners' representative council |
| Schülervertretung | learners' representative council |
| Schulfach | school subject |
| Schulfonds | school development fund |
| Schulgeld | tuition fees, payment of tuition |
| Schulgeldermäßigung | reduction of school fees |
| schulischer Fortschritt | academic progress |
| Schulklinik | school clinic |
| Schulkomitee | school board |
| Schulleiter(in) | headmaster, headmistress, principal |
| Schulleitung | school management |
| Schulpflicht | compulsory school attendance |
| Schulpolitik | education policy, educational policy |

| | |
|---|---|
| Schulreifetest | school readiness test |
| Schulterminkalender | annual school calendar |
| Schulverwaltung | school management/administration |
| Schulverweis | expulsion/suspension of a learner |
| Schulvorstand | school board, controlling body of a school |
| Schulzeugnis | school report |
| Schwellenwert (bei Noteneinstufung) | grade threshold |
| Seiteneinsteiger | lateral entrant, transfer student |
| Sekundarschulabschluss (vollgültiger) in Namibia | fully acknowledged Senior Secondary School Leaving Certificate |
| Sekundarschulwesen | secondary education |
| Sekundarstufe I | junior secondary school |
| Sekundarstufe II | senior secondary school |
| Sonderpädagogik | special education |
| Sonderschule | special school |
| staatliche Schule | state school, government school |
| staatliche Zuwendung für Schulen | subsidy of schools |
| Staatsschule | state school, government school |
| Ständige Konferenz der Kultusminister der Länder in der Bundesrepublik Deutschland | Standing Conference of the Ministers of Education and Cultural Affairs of the Länder (federal states) in the Federal Republic of Germany |
| Student(in) | student |
| Studieneinrichtung | study institution |
| Studiengang | course of study |
| Studienrichtung | field of study |
| studieren | study (to) |
| Studierende(r) vor dem ersten akademischen Abschluss (Grad), ohne akademischen Abschluss (Grad) | undergraduate |
| Studierende(r) | student |
| Studium | study |

| | |
|---|---|
| Studium bis zum Bachelor-Abschluss | undergraduate studies |
| Stufenleiter(in) | head of department (primary, secondary school) |
| Stundenziel | lesson objective |
| Subventionierung der Schulen | subsidy of schools |
| Subventionierung privater Schulen | aid for private schools |
| Suspendierung | expulsion, suspension |
| Syllabus | syllabus |

## T

| | |
|---|---|
| Tagesheim | day-care hostel/centre |
| tertiärer Bildungssektor | tertiary education |
| Test | test, class test |

## U

| | |
|---|---|
| Universität Namibia | University of Namibia (UNAM) |
| Universitätsausbildung | higher education, university education |
| Universitätsbildung | tertiary education |
| Universitätspräsident(in) | Chancellor (of the University of Namibia) |
| Universitätsreife | university exemption |
| Universitätszulassungsberechtigung | university exemption *(to have attained the academic standard to enrol at a university)* |
| Unterricht | tuition |
| Unterricht während des Referendariats | practical teaching |
| Unterricht zu Hause | home schooling |
| Unterrichtsentwurf | lesson plan |
| Unterrichtsgebühren | tuition fees |
| Unterrichtsmaterialien | educational material |
| Unterrichtsmedien | teaching media |
| Unterrichtsplan | lesson plan |
| Unterrichtspraktikum | teaching practice |

| | |
|---|---|
| Unterrichtspraktikum | practical teaching |
| Unterrichtssprache | medium of instruction |
| Unterrichtsverweis | suspension of a learner |
| Unterrichtsvorbereitung | lesson preparation |
| Unterrichtsziel | lesson objective, learning objective |
| Unterstützung von Lernenden | learner support |
| Urkunde | document, certificate, diploma |
| Urkundenbeweis | documentary evidence |

## V

| | |
|---|---|
| Verfügbarkeit von Lehrenden | provision of teachers |
| verbindlicher Lehrplan | core curriculum |
| Verhaltenskodex | general rules of behaviour/conduct, code of conduct |
| Verhaltenskodex (für Lernende) | (learners') code of conduct |
| Verhaltensregeln (für Lernende) | (learners') code of conduct |
| Vertrauenslehrer(in) | confidante, liaison teacher |
| verwehrt (Zulassung) | (admission) refused |
| verweigert (Zulassung) | (admission) refused |
| Vor- und Grundschulerziehung | junior education |
| Vorgehensweise | approach |
| Vorlesung | lecture |
| Vorstand | board of directors, school board |

## Z

| | |
|---|---|
| Zahlung der Unterrichtsgebühren | payment of tuition, tuition fees |
| zensieren | grade (to), correct (to), mark (to) |
| Zertifikat | certificate |
| Zeugnis | certificate, report, testimonial |
| Zulassung (von Lernenden) | admission of learners |
| Zulassungsantrag | application for admission |

| | |
|---|---|
| Zulassungsbedingungen | admission requirements, conditions for admission |
| Zulassungsprüfung | access test, entrance exam |
| zusätzlicher Unterricht | extra classes, extra lessons |
| Zuschuss | subsidy |
| Zuteilung von Lehrkräften | provision of teachers |
| zwangloses Lernen | informal learning |
| Zweitkorrektor(in) | moderator |
| Zweitprüfer(in) | moderator |

# Alltagspolitik und Ministerien

# Everyday Politics and Ministries

## A

| | |
|---|---|
| Abschätzungsverzeichnis | valuation roll |
| Agrarstatistik | agricultural statistics |
| Agrikultur | agriculture |
| aktive Förderungsmaßnahmen | affirmative action |
| Amt des Premierministers (der Premierministerin) | Office of the Prime Minister |
| amtlicher Nachweis der Staatsangehörigkeit/-bürgerschaft | citizenship documents |
| Aquakultur | aquaculture, freshwater and marine |
| Arbeitnehmerhaftpflichtversicherung | employees compensation fund |
| Arbeitsaufsichtsamt, -behörde | labour inspectorate |
| Arbeitsforschungsinstitut | Labour Resource and Research Institute (LaRRI) |
| Arbeitsgruppe | task force, team, workshop |
| Arbeitsinspektor(in) | labour inspector |
| Arbeitskommissar(in) | labour commissioner |
| Arbeitskommission | labour commission |
| Arbeitsrecht | labour legislation |
| Arbeitstagung | workshop, conference |
| Ausbau von Kapazitäten | capacity building |
| ausschließliche Wirtschaftszone | exclusive processing zone |
| Ausschreibung | invitation to tender, call for tender, advertisement |
| Ausschuss zur Vergabe von Farmland | land board |
| Außenministerium | Ministry of Foreign Affairs |
| Ausstand | strike, wild cat strike |
| Auswärtiges Amt | Ministry of Foreign Affairs |

## B

| | |
|---|---|
| Babyentsorgung | baby dumping |
| Beauftragte(r) für Arbeitsrecht | labour commissioner |
| Behörde zur Vergabe von Farmland | land board |
| Beirat | advisory committee |
| Berufsbildungszentrum | Vocational Training Centre |
| Berufsschule (handwerklich) | Vocational Training Centre, vocational school |
| Bildungsministerium | Ministry of Education |
| Bodenabschätzung und Besteuerung | land valuation and taxation |
| Bodenpolitik | land policy |
| Bodenreform | land reform |
| Bodensteuer | land tax |

## C

| | |
|---|---|
| Chief, weiblicher Chief | Chief |

## D

| | |
|---|---|
| Dachverband Namibischer Nichtregierungsorganisationen | Namibia Non-Governmental Organisations Forum Trust (NANGOF Trust) |
| Dezentralisierungsprozess | decentralisation process |
| durchgängige Gleichstellungsorientierung | gender mainstreaming |

## E

| | |
|---|---|
| Einnahmekartell der Zollunion Südliches Afrika | SACU Revenue Pool |
| Energieversorgungskartell Südliches Afrika | Southern African Power Pool (SAPP) |
| Entwicklungsgemeinschaft Südliches Afrika (ESA) | Southern African Development Community (SADC) |
| Erlaubnis | permission, permit |

| | |
|---|---|
| Erlaubnisschein | permit |
| Exportverarbeitungszone | export processing zone (EPZ) |

## F

| | |
|---|---|
| Fahrzeugunfallfonds | Motor Vehicle Accident Fund (MVA Fund) |
| Farmlandsteuer | land tax |
| Finanzministerium | Ministry of Finance |
| Fischfarmerei | fish farming |
| Fischzucht | fish farming |
| Fördermaßnahmen zugunsten benachteiligter Gruppen | affirmative action |

## G

| | |
|---|---|
| gemeindebasiert | community based |
| Gemeindeebene (auf) | community based |
| Gemeinschaftsebene (auf) | community based |
| Gemeinsame Kulturkommission | Joint Commission of Culture |
| Gemeinsame Verteidigungs- und Sicherheitskommission | Joint Commission on Defence and Security |
| Genehmigung | permit, licence, authorization |
| Generalbilanzprüfer(in) | Auditor General |
| Generalbuchprüfer(in) | Auditor General |
| Generalinspekteur(in) | Inspector General |
| Generalwirtschaftsprüfer(in) | Auditor General |
| Geologisches Landesamt | Geological Survey of Namibia |
| Gewerbeaufsichtsamt | labour inspectorate |
| Gewerbeaufsichtsperson, Gewerbeaufseher(in) | labour inspector |
| Gewerkschaftsdachverband Namibias | National Union of Namibian Workers |
| Gewohnheitsrecht | customary right, common law |
| Gewohnheitsrecht auf Grund und Boden | customary land rights |

## H

| | |
|---|---|
| Heldenfriedhof | Heroes Acre |
| Heldengedenkstätte | Heroes Acre |

## I

| | |
|---|---|
| illegaler Streik | illegal strike |
| Industrie- und Handelsministerium | Ministry of Trade and Industry |
| Innenministerium | Ministry of Home Affairs and Immigration |
| Institut für Politikforschung | Institute for Public Policy Research (IPPR) |

## J

| | |
|---|---|
| Justizministerium | Ministry of Justice |

## K

| | |
|---|---|
| Katastrophenhilfe | disaster relief |
| Katastrophenschutz | disaster control |
| Kommission für den öffentlichen Dienst | Public Service Commission (PSC) |
| Kommission zur Gleichstellung am Arbeitsplatz | Employment Equity Commission |
| Kompetenzförderung | capacity building |
| Korrekturmaßnahmen | affirmative action |
| korrigierende Maßnahmen | affirmative action |

## L

| | |
|---|---|
| Landesamt für Geologie | Geological Survey of Namibia |
| ländliche Wasserversorgung | communal management of rural water supply |
| Landwirtschaft | agriculture |
| Landwirtschaftlicher Arbeitgeberverband (LAV) | Agricultural Employers Association (AEA) |

| | |
|---|---|
| landwirtschaftlicher Berater(in) | agricultural extension officer |
| Landwirtschaftlicher Beratungsdienst | agricultural extension services |
| Landwirtschaftsstatistik | agricultural statistics |
| Leitzins (-satz) | prime lending rate |

| | |
|---|---|
| Maßnahmen zur Chancengleichheit | affirmative action |
| medizinische Grundversorgung | primary health care |
| Ministerium des Präsidialamts/für Präsidentschaftsangelegenheiten | Ministry of Presidential Affairs |
| Ministerium für Arbeit und Soziales | Ministry of Labour and Social Welfare |
| Ministerium für Bergbau und Energie | Ministry of Mines and Energy |
| Ministerium für Geschlechtergleichheit und Kinderfürsorge | Ministry of Gender Equality and Child Welfare |
| Ministerium für Gesundheit und Sozialleistungen | Ministry of Health and Social Services |
| Ministerium für Hochseefischerei und Meeresressourcen | Ministry of Fisheries and Marine Resources |
| Ministerium für Information und Kommunikationstechnologie | Ministry of Information and Communication Technology |
| Ministerium für Innere Sicherheit | Ministry of Safety and Security |
| Ministerium für Jugend, Wehrdienst, Sport und Kultur | Ministry of Youth, National Service, Sport and Culture |
| Ministerium für Kommunal- und Regionalverwaltung, Wohnungsbau und ländliche Entwicklung | Ministry of Regional and Local Government, Housing and Rural Development |
| Ministerium für Kriegsveteranen | Ministry of Veteran Affairs |
| Ministerium für Landfragen und Neubesiedlung | Ministry of Lands and Resettlement |
| Ministerium für öffentliche Arbeiten und Verkehr | Ministry of Works and Transport |
| Ministerium für Umwelt und Touristik | Ministry of Environment and Tourism |
| Ministerium für Wasserversorgung, Land- und Forstwirtschaft | Ministry of Agriculture, Water and Forestry |

# N

| | |
|---|---|
| Nachtragshaushalt | additional budget |
| Namibische Akademie für Touristik und Gastgewerbe | Namibian Academy for Tourism and Hospitality (NATH) |
| Namibische Bauarbeitergewerkschaft | Namibia Building Workers Union (NABWU) |
| Namibische Bergarbeitergewerkschaft | Mine Workers Union of Namibia |
| Namibische Börse | Namibian Stock Exchange (NSX) |
| Namibische Bus- und Taxivereinigung | Namibia Bus and Taxi Association (NABTA) |
| Namibische Dienstleistungsgewerkschaft | Public Service Union of Namibia (PSUN) |
| Namibische Farmarbeitergewerkschaft | Namibia Farm Workers Union (NAFWU) |
| Namibische Fischindustriegewerkschaft | Namibia Fishing Industries and Fishermen Workers Union (Namfish) |
| Namibische Flughafengesellschaft | Namibia Airport Company (NAC) |
| Namibische Gewerkschaft der Kommunalfarmer | Namibia National Farmers Union (NNFU) |
| Namibische Gewerkschaft für Angestellte der Nahrungsmittelindustrie | Namibian Food and Allied Workers Union (NAFAU) |
| Namibische Gewerkschaft für Angestellte des öffentlichen Dienstes | Namibia Public Workers Union (NAPWU) |
| Namibische Gewerkschaft für Angestellte im Groß- und Einzelhandel | Namibia Wholesale and Retail Workers Union (NWRWU) |
| Namibische Gewerkschaft für Metallindustriearbeiter(innen) | Metal and Allied Namibian Workers Union |
| Namibische Gewerkschaft für Stadtverwaltungsangestellte | Local Authorities Union of Namibia |
| Namibische Industrie- und Handelskammer | Namibian Chamber of Commerce and Industry (NCCI) |
| Namibische Juristenvereinigung | Law Society of Namibia |
| Namibische Kontrollbehörde für Finanzinstitute | Namibia Financial Institutions Supervisory Authority (NAMFISA) |
| Namibische Krebsvereinigung | Cancer Association of Namibia (CAN) |

| | |
|---|---|
| Namibische Mineralölgesellschaft | National Petroleum Corporation of Namibia (NAMCOR) |
| Namibische Nationale Lehrergewerkschaft | Namibia National Teachers Union (NANTU) |
| Namibische Naturparks | Namibia Wildlife Resorts (NWR) |
| Namibische Qualifizierungsbehörde | Namibian Qualifications Authority (NQA) |
| Namibische Rechtsreform- und Entwicklungskommission | Law Reform and Development Commission of Namibia |
| Namibische Touristikbehörde | Namibia Tourism Board (NTB) |
| Namibische Vereinigung der Rechtsassistenten(-innen) | Namibia Paralegal Association (NPA) |
| Namibische Vereinigung für Recht und Verantwortung | Namibian Rights and Responsibilities Inc. (NAMRIGHTS) |
| Namibische Verteidigung/Streitkräfte/Streitmacht/Armee | Namibian Defence Force (NDF) |
| Namibische Wahlkommission | Electoral Commission of Namibia (ECN) |
| Namibische Zentralbank | Bank of Namibia (BoN) |
| Namibische Zentralstelle für die Anerkennung von Bildungsabschlüssen | Namibian Qualifications Authority (NQA) |
| Namibischer Arbeitgeberverband | Namibian Employers' Federation (NEF) |
| Namibischer Berufsjagdverband | Namibia Professional Hunting Association (NAPHA) |
| Namibischer Gastgewerbeverband | Hospitality Association of Namibia (HAN) |
| Namibischer Kirchenrat | Council of Churches in Namibia (CCN) |
| Namibischer Landwirtschaftsverband | Namibia Agricultural Union (NAU) |
| Namibischer Produzentenverband | Namibian Manufacturers Association (NMA) |
| Namibischer Tour- und Safariunternehmerverband | Tour and Safari Association of Namibia (TASA) |
| Namibischer Touristikdachverband | Federation of Namibian Tourism Associations (FENATA) |
| Namibischer Touristikrat | Namibia Tourism Board (NTB) |
| Namibischer Verband der Kommunalfarmer | Namibia National Farmers Union (NNFU) |

| | |
|---|---|
| Namibischer Verband für Touristik auf Gemeindeebene/für gemeindebasierte Touristik | Namibia Community Based Tourism Association (NACOBTA) |
| Namibisches Institut für Normung | Namibia Standards Institution (NSI) |
| Nationalarchiv | National Archives |
| Nationalbibliothek | National Library of Namibia |
| Nationale Planungskommission | National Planning Commission |
| Nationale Prüfungsbehörde | Department of National Examinations and Assessment (DNEA) |
| Nationaler Hochschulrat | National Council for Higher Education (NCHE) |
| Nationaler Verkehrssicherheitsrat | National Road Safety Council (NRSC) |
| Nationales Institut für Bildungsentwicklung | National Institute for Educational Development (NIED) |
| Nationalgalerie | National Art Gallery |
| Nationalmuseum | National Museum of Namibia |
| Notfallmanagement | Emergency Management Unit |

## P

| | |
|---|---|
| Parlamentspräsident(in) | Speaker of Parliament |
| Pensionsfonds staatlicher Institutionen | Government Institutions Pension Fund (GIPF) |
| Permit | permit |
| Politik | policy, politics |
| Präsidialamt | Office of the President |
| Pressekonferenz | media conference, press conference |
| Programm | programme, policy |
| Programm zur Förderung schwarzen Unternehmertums | black economic empowerment |

## R

| | |
|---|---|
| Rahmenbedingungen | policy framework, regulatory framework |
| Rahmenrichtlinien | policy framework, regulatory framework |

| | |
|---|---|
| Rat zur Vergabe von Farmland | land board |
| Regionalrat | regional council |
| reproduktive Gesundheit | reproductive health |
| Richtlinie | guide line, directives, policy |
| Richtlinienplanung | policy planning |

## S

| | |
|---|---|
| Sekretariat des Aufsichtsrates für Staatsunternehmen | State Owned Enterprises Governing Council Secretariat |
| Sozialversicherung | Social Security Commission (SSC) |
| Speaker des Parlaments | Speaker of Parliament |
| Staatsangehörigkeit | citizenship |
| Staatsbürgerschaft | citizenship |
| Staatssekretär(in) | Permanent Secretary |
| Stammesgesetze und Gebräuche | traditional laws and practices |
| Ständiger Parlamentsausschuss für öffentliche Ausgaben/Bilanzen | Parliamentary Standing Committee on Public Accounts |
| Straßenbaubehörde | Roads Authority |
| Straßenbaufirma | road construction company |
| Straßenbaufonds | Road Fund Administration (RFA) |
| Straßenbauunternehmen | Roads Contractor Company (RCC) |
| Strategie | strategy, policy |
| Strategieplanung | policy planning, strategic planning |

## T

| | |
|---|---|
| Tender | tender |
| Touristikmesse | Tourism Expo |

## U

| | |
|---|---|
| Umwelt- und Touristikministerium | Ministry of Environment and Tourism |
| Unterstaatssekretär(in) | Undersecretary |

## V

| | |
|---|---|
| Vergabebehörde | Tender Board |
| Verteidigungsministerium | Ministry of Defence |

## W

| | |
|---|---|
| Wertschöpfung | value adding |
| widerrechtlicher Streik | illegal strike |
| wilder Streik | illegal strike |
| wirtschaftliche Stärkung der schwarzen Bevölkerung | black economic empowerment |
| Wirtschaftsbearbeitungszone | economic processing zone |
| Workshop | workshop |

## Z

| | |
|---|---|
| Zentrale Vergabestelle | Tender Board |
| Zollunion Südliches Afrika (ZUSA) | South African Custom Union (SACU) |

# Rechtswesen | Law and Related Matters

## A

| | |
|---|---|
| Abfindung | severance pay |
| Advokat(in) | advocate |
| amtierende(r) Richter(in) | acting judge |
| Amtsblatt | Government Gazette |
| Amtsrichter(in) | Magistrate |
| Änderung des Gesetzes | amendment of law |
| anhängiger Streitgegenstand | pending dispute |
| Ankläger(in) | prosecutor |
| Anwalt (Anwältin) | lawyer, attorney, advocate |
| Arbeitsbedingungen | basic working conditions |
| Arbeitsbescheinigung | certificate of employment |
| Arbeitsgericht | labour court |
| Arbeitsnachweis | certificate of employment |
| Aufhebung des Gesetzes | repeal of law |
| Aussperrung | lock-out |

## B

| | |
|---|---|
| Beendigung des Arbeitsverhältnisses durch Kündigung | termination of employment on notice |
| Berufungsverfahren | appeal hearing |
| Beurlaubung | leave of absence |
| Beweis | evidence, proof |
| Beweismittel | piece of evidence |
| Bezahlung | remuneration, payment |

## D

| | |
|---|---|
| Dauer des Angestelltenverhältnisses | period of employment |
| Disput | dispute |

| | |
|---|---|
| Disziplinarverfahren | disciplinary hearing |

## E

| | |
|---|---|
| Entlassungsabfindung | severance pay |
| Erziehungsurlaub | maternity leave (paternity leave) |

## F

| | |
|---|---|
| faire Verfahrensregeln | code of good practice |

## G

| | |
|---|---|
| Gehalt | salary |
| Generalstaatsanwalt (-anwältin) | Attorney General, Prosecutor General |
| Gerichtspräsident(in) | Judge President |
| gesetzliche Vorschrift | provisions of act |
| Gewerkschaft | trade union |
| Gewohnheitsrechtreform | customary law reform |
| Grundrechte | fundamental rights and protections |

## H

| | |
|---|---|
| Haftbarkeit | liability |
| Haftpflicht | liability |
| Haftung | liability, responsibility |

## J

| | |
|---|---|
| Jahresurlaub | annual leave |
| Jurist(in) | lawyer |
| juristische Handhabung | instruments of law |
| juristische Rechtsmittel | right of appeal, means of legal redress |

## K

| | |
|---|---|
| Koalitionsfreiheit | freedom of association |
| Konfliktbeilegung | resolution of disputes |
| Kontroverse | conflict, controversy, dispute |

| | |
|---|---|
| Krankheitsurlaub | sick leave |
| Krankschreibung | sick leave |

## L

| | |
|---|---|
| Lohnerhöhung | wage increase |
| Lohnforderung | wage demand |
| Lohnpolitik | wage policy |
| Lohnverhandlung | wage negotiation |

## M

| | |
|---|---|
| Magistrat(in) | Magistrate |
| Magistratsgericht | Magistrate's Court |

## N

| | |
|---|---|
| Nachtarbeit | night work |
| Nachtschicht | night shift |
| Novelle | amendment of law |
| novellieren | amend (to) |

## O

| | |
|---|---|
| Obergericht | High Court |
| Oberrichter | Chief Justice |
| Oberster Gerichtshof | Supreme Court |

## R

| | |
|---|---|
| Rechtsanwalt (-anwältin) | barrister, lawyer, attorney |
| Rechtsassistent(in) ohne formaljuristische Ausbildung | paralegal |
| Rechtsbeistandszentrum | Legal Assistance Centre (LAC) |
| Rechtshilfezentrum | Legal Assistance Centre (LAC) |
| Rechtsreform, Gesetzesreform und Entwicklungsausschuss | Law Reform and Development Commission |
| Rechtsspruch | judgement |

| | |
|---|---|
| Revision | amendment, appeal, revision, audit |
| Revisionsverfahren | appeal hearing |
| Richter(in) | judge |

## S

| | |
|---|---|
| Schlichtung | conciliation |
| Schlichtung, -sverfahren | arbitration |
| Sonderurlaub aufgrund eines Todes-/Trauerfalls | compassionate leave |
| Staatsankläger(in) | Prosecutor General |
| Staatsanzeiger | Government Gazette |
| stellvertretende(r) Richter(in) | acting judge |
| strafrechtliche Verfolgung | prosecution |

## T

| | |
|---|---|
| Tariffestsetzung | wage order |
| Tarifkommission | wage commission |
| Tarifverhandlung | wage negotiation |

## U

| | |
|---|---|
| Übergangslösung | resolution of transitional matters |
| Urteil | judgement, verdict |

## V

| | |
|---|---|
| Verbindlichkeit | liability, obligation |
| Vereinigungsfreiheit | freedom of association |
| Verfassungsgericht | Supreme Court |
| Vergütung | payment, reimbursement, remuneration |
| Verkündung eines (vom Parlament verabschiedeten) Gesetzes | Promulgation of Act of Parliament |
| verlängerter Mutterschaftsurlaub | extended maternity leave |
| Versammlungsfreiheit | freedom of assembly |

| | |
|---|---|
| Verteidigung | defence |
| Vorinstanz | lower court |

## W

| | |
|---|---|
| Widerrufung des Gesetzes | repeal of law |

## Z

| | |
|---|---|
| Zuständigkeit und Machtbefugnis des Gerichts | jurisdiction and powers of court |

# Sonderpädagogik | Special Education

## A

| | |
|---|---|
| Abteilung des Erziehungsministeriums, die sich mit Diagnostik, Beratung und Fortbildung befasst | Division: Diagnostic, Advisory and Training Services |
| Abteilung des Erziehungsministeriums, die sich mit Sonderpädagogik befasst | Division: Special Programmes and Schools |
| Akustiker(in) | acoustician |
| allgemeines Schulsystem | mainstream school system |
| Alphabetisierung | literacy |
| Alphabetisierungskampagne | literacy programme |
| angeboren | congenital |
| Aphasie (eine Form der Sprachstörung) | aphasia |
| Arbeitstherapeut(in) | occupational therapist (OT) |
| Audiogramm | audiogram |
| Audiologe (Audiologin) | audiologist *(in Germany they are specialised doctors, in Southern Africa they are paramedical professionals)* |
| Audiologie | audiology |
| Audiometer<br>  - für Aussonderungsuntersuchungen<br>  - zur Messung von Luft- und Knochenleitung | audiometer<br>  - screening audiometer<br>  - diagnostic audiometer |
| auditive Wahrnehmung | auditory perception |
| auditive Wahrnehmungsstörung | auditory perception problem |
| Autismus | autism |
| autistisch (ein Mensch mit Autismus) | autistic |

## B

| | |
|---|---|
| Basis | grass roots |
| Basisansatz | grass root level |
| Basisebene | grass root level |

| | |
|---|---|
| behindert | disabled |
| Behinderte(r) | person with disabilities |
| Behindertenfragen | disability issues |
| Behindertenorganisation | organisation of persons with disabilities |
| Behinderung | disability, handicap |
| beidseitig gelähmt | paraplegic |
| benachteiligt<br>- in kultureller Hinsicht<br>- in pädagogischer Hinsicht<br>- in sozialer Hinsicht | disadvantaged<br>- culturally<br>- educationally<br>- socially |
| Beschäftigungstherapeut(in) | occupational therapist |
| besondere Bedürfnisse | special needs |
| Betreuungslehrer(in) | peripatetic teacher (specialised traveling teacher) |
| Blindenschrift | Braille |

## C

| | |
|---|---|
| Cochlea Implantat (CI) | cochlear implant (CI) |

## D

| | |
|---|---|
| Dachorganisation der Behinderten (behinderter Menschen) | National Federation of People with Disabilities (NFPDN) |
| Dachorganisation der Sehbehinderten | National Federation of the Visually Impaired (NFVI) |
| doppelseitig gelähmt | paraplegic |
| Down-Syndrom | Down syndrome |
| Dyskalkulie | dyscalculia |

## E

| | |
|---|---|
| einseitig gelähmt | hemiplegic |
| emotionale Störung | emotional difficulty |
| ergebnisorientiert | outcome oriented |
| Ergotherapeut(in) | occupational therapist (OT), ergotherapist |

## F

| | |
|---|---|
| Förderschule | special school |
| frühkindliche Entwicklung | early childhood development (ECD) |
| Funktionsbeeinträchtigung | disability, functional disorder, dysfunction |
| Funktionsstörung | disability, functional disorder |

## G

| | |
|---|---|
| Gebärdensprachdolmetscher(in) | sign language interpreter |
| gehörlos | deaf |
| geistig behindert | mentally challenged |
| geschützte/beschützende Werkstätte | sheltered workshop |
| geschützte Beschäftigung | sheltered employment |
| Gesundheitswesen, im Gesundheitswesen Tätige | health, health professionals |
| Großdruck | big, enlarged print |

## H

| | |
|---|---|
| halbseitig gelähmt | hemiplegic |
| Hilfsorganisation für Kinder mit Behinderungen | CHAIN (Children with Handicaps – Action in Namibia) |
| Hilfsorganisation für Kinder mit Hör-, Sprach- und Sprechstörungen | CLaSH (The Association for Children with Language, Speech and Hearing Impairments of Namibia) |
| Hirnhautentzündung | meningitis |
| HNO (Hals-Nasen-Ohren) | ENT (Ear, Nose and Throat) |
| hochbegabt | gifted |
| Hörgerät<br>  - Hinter-dem Ohr-Gerät<br>  - Im-Ohr-Gerät<br>  - Taschengerät | hearing aid<br>  - behind-the-ear aid<br>  - in-the-ear aid<br>  - pocket aid |
| hörgeschädigt | hearing impaired |
| Hörsturz | sudden hearing loss |

| | |
|---|---|
| Hörverlust | hearing loss |
| - leicht | - mild |
| - mittelgradig | - moderate |
| - hochgradig | - severe |
| - total | - profound |

## I

| | |
|---|---|
| Inklusive Pädagogik | Inclusive Education (IE) |
| Innenohrschaden | sensorineural hearing loss |
| integrativer Unterricht | integration |

## K

| | |
|---|---|
| Kooperationslehrer(in) | peripatetic teacher (specialised traveling teacher) |
| körperbehindert | physically disabled |
| Krankengymnast(in) | physiotherapist |

## L

| | |
|---|---|
| Legasthenie | dyslexia |
| Legastheniker(in) | (he/she is) dyslexic |
| leistungsabhängig | performance-based |
| Lernbehinderung | learning disability |
| Lernschwäche | learning difficulty |
| Lernstörung | learning disability |
| Lese-Rechtschreibschwäche | dyslexia |
| Logopäde (Logopädin) | speech and language therapist (SLT) |

## M

| | |
|---|---|
| Mehrfachbehinderung | multiple disabilities |
| Meningitis | meningitis |
| Mittelohrentzündung | middle ear infection (= otitis media) |
| Muskeltonus | muscle tone |
| - herabgesetzte Muskelspannung (hypoton) | - low |
| - übersteigerte Muskelspannung (hyperton) | - high |

| | |
|---|---|
| Namibische Gebärdensprache | Namibian Sign Language (NSL) |
| Namibische Vereinigung der Gehörlosen | Namibia National Association of the Deaf (NNAD) |
| Namibischer Gehörlosenverein | Namibia National Association of the Deaf (NNAD) |

| | |
|---|---|
| Pädagogische(r) und psychologische(r) Berater(in) für Lerner/Schüler(innen) | Regional School Counsellors (RSC) |
| pädagogischer Förderbedarf | additional educational needs (AEN) |
| paramedizinisch (den medizinischen Berufen zugehörig) | paramedical |
| Paukenröhrchen | grommets |
| Physiotherapeut(in) | physiotherapist |
| Prothese | prosthesis |

| | |
|---|---|
| Rechenfähigkeit (mathematische Fähigkeit) | numeracy |
| Rechenschwäche | dyscalculia |
| Regelschulwesen | mainstream school system |
| Richtlinie für den Umgang mit Menschen mit Behinderung | policy on people with disabilities |
| Rollstuhlfahrer(in) | wheelchair user |

S

| | |
|---|---|
| Sanitäter(in) | paramedic |
| Schädigung | impairment |
| - geistige Behinderung | - mental impairment |
| - Hörschädigung, Gehörlosigkeit, Schwerhörigkeit | - hearing impairment |
| - Körperbehinderung | - physical impairment |
| - Sehschädigung, Blindheit, Sehbehinderung | - visual impairment |
| - Sinnesschädigung | - sensory impairment |
| - Sprechbehinderung, Sprachbehinderung | - speech, language impairment |

| | |
|---|---|
| Schreib- und Lesefähigkeit | literacy |
| schwerhörig | hard-of-hearing |
| sonderpädagogische Bedürfnisse | special educational needs (SEN) |
| Sonderschule | special school |
| soziale Beeinträchtigung | social handicap |
| Sprachanbahnung | language stimulation |
| Sprachaudiogramm | speech discrimination test |
| Sprachentwicklung | language development |
| Sprachentwicklungsverzögerung | language delay |
| Sprachstimulation | language stimulation |
| Sprachtherapeut(in) | speech, language therapist (SLT) |
| Sprachtherapie | speech therapy |
| staatliches Institut für Sonderpädagogik | National Institute for Special Education (NISE) |
| stockendes Sprechen | stutter, stammer, disfluent speech |
| Störung | disorder |
| Störung des Gefühlslebens | emotional difficulty |
| stottern | stutter (to), stammer (to) |

## T

| | |
|---|---|
| taub | deaf |
| taubblind | deaf blind |
| technische Hilfen und Geräte | assistive devices |

## U

| | |
|---|---|
| unterstützte Arbeitsplätze | sheltered employment |

## V

| | |
|---|---|
| Verhaltensauffälligkeit | behavioural difficulty |
| Verhaltensstörung | behavioural difficulty/disturbance |
| visuelle Wahrnehmung | visual perception |
| vom Bildungssystem vernachlässigte Kinder | educationally marginalised children |

## W

| | |
|---|---|
| Wahrnehmungsstörung | sensory integration problem |
| Waisen und schutzbedürftige Kinder | Orphans and Vulnerable Children (OVC) |

## Z

| | |
|---|---|
| Zerebralparese | cerebral palsy (CP) |

# Geschlechterfragen | Gender Issues

## A

| | |
|---|---|
| Afrikanische Charta der Menschenrechte | African Charter on Human and Peoples' Rights |
| Afrikanische Rechtsinitiative | All Africa Rights Initiative |
| AIDS Pandemie | AIDS pandemic |
| Anlaufstelle | drop-in centre |
| antiretrovirale Medikamente | anti-retroviral drugs (ARV) |
| AU-Protokoll zu Frauenrechten in Afrika | AU Protocol on the Rights of Women in Africa |
| ausgewogene Verteilung der Haushaltspflichten | equal sharing of domestic responsibilities |
| ausgewogenes Geschlechterverhältnis bei Anstellungen | gender balance of appointments |

## B

| | |
|---|---|
| Brautpreis | bride price, lobola |
| Brüderlichkeit | brotherhood, brotherliness |
| Bruderschaft | brotherhood |
| Bürgerrechtsorganisationen | civil rights awareness organisations |

## D

| | |
|---|---|
| Dienststelle für Gleichstellungsfragen | gender desk |
| durchgängige Gleichstellungsorientierung | gender mainstreaming |

## E

| | |
|---|---|
| Ehegatten-Gleichstellungsgesetz | Married Persons Equality Act 1 of 1996 |
| Eigentumsklau von Witwen | property grabbing from widows |
| Einheit zum Schutz von Frauen und Kindern | Women and Child Protection Unit |

| | |
|---|---|
| Entwicklungsgesellschaft Südliches Afrika Erklärung zur Geschlechter- und Entwicklungspolitik | SADC Protocol and Declaration on Gender and Development |

## F

| | |
|---|---|
| Fehlen des sozialen Zusammenhalts | social cohesion deficit |
| Frauenförderung | women's empowerment |
| Frauennetzwerk an der Basis (auf Basisebene) | grass roots women's network |
| Frauensolidarität | women's solidarity |

## G

| | |
|---|---|
| gemeinsames Sorgerecht und gleichberechtigte Vormundschaft | joint custody and equal guardianship |
| Geschlechter und Medien | Gender and Media (GEM) |
| Geschlechter und Medien Netzwerk Südliches Afrika | Gender and Media Southern Africa Network (GEMSA) |
| geschlechterbezogene/ geschlechtsspezifische Gewalt | gender based violence |
| Geschlechterdynamik | gender dynamics |
| Geschlechterforschungs- und Förderungsprojekt | Gender Research and Advocacy Project |
| Geschlechtergleichheit | gender equality |
| Gesetz zur Bekämpfung häuslicher Gewalt | Domestic Violence Act |
| Gesetz zur Gleichstellung am Arbeitsplatz | Affirmative Action (Employment) Act of 1998 |
| Gesetz zur Unterhaltszahlung | Maintenance Act |
| Gesetz zur Vergewaltigungsbekämpfung | Combating of Rape Act |
| Gesetzesentwurf zur homosexuellen Eheschließung | Bill on Gay Marriages |
| Gesetzesentwurf zur Anerkennung von Stammesehen | Recognition of Customary Marriage Bill |

| | |
|---|---|
| Gesetzesentwurf zur Rechtsstellung von Kindern | Children's Status Bill |
| gleichgeschlechtliche Ehe | same sex marriage |
| Gleichstellung von Frauen und Männern | gender equality |
| Gleichstellungsbarometer im Südlichen Afrika | Southern Africa Gender Justice Barometer |
| gleichstellungsbezogene Gesetzgebung | gender-related legislation |
| Gleichstellungsetat | gender budgeting |
| Gleichstellungspolitik (Richtlinien der Geschlechter) | gender policies |
| Gleichstellungsrechtfertigung | gender justification |
| Gleichstellungsschulungs- und Forschungsprogramm der Universität Namibia | University of Namibia's Gender Training and Research Programme |
| Gleichstellungssensibilitätstraining | gender sensitivity training |
| globale Ungleichheit | global inequality |

## H

| | |
|---|---|
| Homoehe | same sex marriage |

## I

| | |
|---|---|
| Internationale Menschenrechtsbewegung der Schwulen und Lesben | International Gay and Lesbian Human Rights Movement |
| Internationales Netzwerk für soziale Gerechtigkeit, Frieden, Umweltschutz, Menschenrechte durch die Bereitstellung von Kommunikations-Infrastruktur | Association for Progressive Communications Women's Networking Support Programme (APC WNSP) |

## K

| | |
|---|---|
| Kinderbetreuungs- und Kinderschutzgesetz | Child Care and Protection Act |
| Kinderehe | child marriage |

| | |
|---|---|
| Kindweibehe | child marriage |
| Kommission zur Gleichstellung am Arbeitsplatz | Employment Equity Commission |
| Kongress zur Beseitigung aller Diskriminierung von Frauen | Convention on the Elimination of All Forms of Discrimination Against Women (CEDAW) |
| kulturabhängige Gewohnheiten | cultural practices |
| kulturelle Bräuche | cultural practices |

## M

| | |
|---|---|
| Männerverehrung | male worshipping |
| Mehrehe | polygamy |
| Menschenhandel | human trafficking |
| Menschenrechte von Frauen | women's human rights |
| Mitgiftverbrechen | dowry crimes |

## N

| | |
|---|---|
| Namibische Demographie- und Gesundheitsumfrage | Namibian Demographic and Health Survey |
| Namibischer Verein für Familienplanung | Namibia Planned Parenthood Association (NAPPA) |
| Namibisches Frauenmanifest-Netzwerk | Namibian Women's Manifesto Network |
| Nationaler Exekutivausschuss des namibischen NGO Forums (NANGOF) für Geschlechterfragen | National Executive Committee of the Namibian NGO Forum (NANGOF) Gender Sector |

## O

| | |
|---|---|
| Opferbetreuung (Programm zur Opferbetreuung) | Victim Support (Programme) |

## P

| | |
|---|---|
| politische und wirtschaftliche Handlungsfähigkeit der Frauen | women's political and economic empowerment |
| Polygamie | polygamy |

| | |
|---|---|
| Postexpositionsprophylaxe zur Verhütung einer HIV-Infektion | post-exposure prophylaxis to reduce chances of HIV-infection (PEP) |
| Programm zur Verhütung der HIV Übertragung von Eltern auf Kinder | Prevention of Parent to Child Transmission Programme (of HIV) |

## R

| | |
|---|---|
| Rechte sexueller Minderheiten | rights of sexual minorities |
| Rechte von Mädchen und Frauen | rights of girls and women |

## S

| | |
|---|---|
| Scheidungsgesetz | Divorce Act |
| Schwesterlichkeit | sisterhood |
| Schwesternschaft (Nonnen) | sisterhood |
| Selbstbestimmung der Frauen | women's empowerment |
| Sextourismus | sex trafficking of women and girls |
| Sexualhandel von Frauen und Mädchen | sex trafficking of women and girls |
| sexuell ausnutzen | take sexual advantage (to) |
| sexuell belästigen | molest sexually (to) |
| sexuelle und fortpflanzungsbezogene Rechte | sexual and reproductive rights |
| Solidarität von Frauen | women's solidarity |
| soziales Zusammenhaltsdefizit | social cohesion deficit |
| Stammesehe | customary marriage |
| Strafverfahren und Änderungsgesetz | Criminal Procedure and Amendment Act |

## T

| | |
|---|---|
| Teilnahme von Frauen an Entscheidungsprozessen fördern | promote women's participation (to) |
| Transsexuelle | transgender people |

## U

| | |
|---|---|
| unkooperative Eltern | unsupportive parents |
| Unterhaltsermittler | maintenance investigator |
| unterschiedliche Formen des Zusammenlebens | different forms of co-habitation |

## V

| | |
|---|---|
| verantwortungsbewusste (gute) Regierungsführung | good governance |
| Vergötterung des männlichen Geschlechts | male worshipping |
| Verhältniswahlsystem, Verhältniswahl (in der Gesetzgebung und bei Gemeindewahlen) | Proportional Representation (PR) System (in legislation and local elections) |
| verletzliche Zeugen | vulnerable witnesses |
| Verletzung der sexuellen Rechte der Frauen | violation of women's sexual rights |
| verschiedene (unterschiedliche) sexuelle Veranlagungen | diverse sexual orientations |
| Vielweiberei | polygamy |

## W

| | |
|---|---|
| weiblich Genitalverstümmelung | female genital mutilation |
| Witwenopferung | widow immolation |
| Witwenverbrennung | widow immolation |

## Z

| | |
|---|---|
| zivilrechtliche Durchsetzungsanstrengung | civil enforcement efforts |

www.ingramcontent.com/pod-product-compliance
Lightning Source LLC
Chambersburg PA
CBHW022228010526
44113CB00033B/739